PLOTINUS
or
The Simplicity of Vision

Bust of Plotinus
photograph from Bibliothèque
nationale, Paris. Courtesy
Giraudon/Art Resource, N.Y.

ꡂꡂꡂ Pierre Hadot ꡄꡄꡄ

PLOTINUS
or
The Simplicity of Vision

Translated by
Michael Chase

With an Introduction by
Arnold I. Davidson

The University of Chicago Press
Chicago and London

Originally published in French as
Plotin ou la simplicité du regard, troisième édition,
by Institut des Etudes Augustiniennes, 1989.

The University of Chicago Press, Chicago 60637
The University of Chicago Press, Ltd., London
© 1993 by The University of Chicago
All rights reserved. Published 1993
Paperback edition 1998
Printed in the United States of America

02 01 00 99 98   2 3 4 5
ISBN 0-226-31193-7 (cloth)
ISBN 0-226-31194-5 (paper)

Library of Congress Cataloging-in-Publication Data

Hadot, Pierre.
  [Plotin ou la simplicité du regard. English]
  Plotinus, or The simplicity of vision / Pierre Hadot ; translated
by Michael Chase ; with an introduction by Arnold I. Davidson.
      p.   cm.
  Includes bibliographical references and index.
  1. Plotinus. I. Title. II. Title: Simplicity of vision.
B693.Z7H2813   1993
186'.4—dc20   93-25166
                                                   CIP

♾ The paper used in this publication meets the minimum
requirements of the American National Standard for
Information Sciences—Permanence of Paper for Printed
Library Materials, ANSI Z39.48-1984.

To the memory
of my friend
G. H. de Radkowski,
who asked me to write this book
in 1963

Contents

Translator's Preface

The best translator is one who makes his presence barely noticeable. I do not feel I have met this standard, and therefore ask the reader's indulgence for a few words of self-justification.

This was not an easy book to translate. Since I have the honor of being a friend as well as a disciple of the author, I wanted to do my very best to prove Nabokov wrong, and produce a *traduzione* which would not be the act of a *traditore*. In some respects this was a quixotic hope right from the start, for the following reasons:

Hadot wrote this book in 1963, and though it has since gone through three editions in France, the last one in 1989, the author has not altered it substantially since then. This caused me no difficulty for the body of the text; all I had to do was to try to reproduce the brisk, informal, enthusiastic tone in which the book was written. Problems arose, however, when it came to the quotations from Plotinus. When Hadot wrote, he used the best edition of Plotinus available at that time: that of Emile Bréhier, whose translations he occasionally altered slightly. Since 1963, however, there has been an explosion of editions, translations, and commentaries of Plotinus, as the reader can tell from a glance at Hadot's Analytical Bibliography. To make a long story short, Bréhier's Greek text, never very reliable, has been made obsolete by the editions of Henry and Schwyzer, while his translation—once characterized by Paul Henry as "one of the clearest in the Budé collection, but not one of the most accurate"—has since been surpassed by translations and commentaries in German, English, and Spanish. That, in spite of this proliferation, work on the translation of Plotinus still needs to be done is indicated by the fact that Hadot himself has begun the enormous task of retranslating and commenting on all of Plotinus' *Enneads*.

The result of this state of affairs is that many of Bréhier's translations—and therefore also the citations given by Hadot—are now held by modern scholarship to be less than accurate. What was a translator to do?

After much conscience-wrestling and consultation with Hadot himself, I decided the only solution was to retranslate the Plotinus quotations myself, from the Greek edition of Henry/Schwyzer. My procedure was as follows: in the case of each quotation from Plotinus, I would first translate the Hadot/Bréhier version into literal English. I then compared this version with the Greek text, and if there were no significant differences, I left it alone. When there were important divergences, however—and this happened more often than not—I came up with my own translation, after consulting the translations and commentaries of Harder/Theiler/Beutler,[1] Armstrong, Igal (in the case of *Enneads* I–IV), and Bouillet (occasionally),[2] and the *Lexicon* of Sleeman and Pollet. In the case of quotations from *Ennead* VI 7 (45), my task was the easy one of rendering Hadot's own meticulously accurate translation, and in the case of *Ennead* VI 8 (39), I was likewise able to benefit from the scholarly efforts of Georges Leroux.[3]

But I did not stop there. I have added a number of footnotes:[4] some explain the identity of persons, places, and writings familiar to a European audience but perhaps less so to an American public. Others give information on historical personages, and still others— these are the ones it is most difficult for me to justify—are intended to help in the understanding of the Plotinus quotations themselves, either by briefly explaining tricky points of doctrine or by pointing out quotations and images taken mostly from Plato.

Above all, I want to avoid giving the impression that I think I know more about Plotinus than the author. Even in 1963, Hadot was perfectly capable of tracking down allusions to Platonic texts, and if he chose not to do so it was for a reason. His reason was, I think, quite simply, that he did not wish his *Plotinus* to be a work of scholarship. In the postface to the second edition (1973), Hadot explained his procedure as follows:

1. Indicated in my footnotes by the abbreviation H/T/B.
2. *Les Ennéades de Plotin, chef de l'école néoplatonicienne, traduites pour la première fois en français* . . . by M.-N. Bouillet, 3 vols., Paris: Hachette, 1857–61.
3. On all these works, see the Analytical Bibliography, below, 125–27.
4. My footnotes—always designated as such and enclosed in brackets—are to be distinguished from those added by Hadot.

I have changed nothing of the text of this little essay. No doubt it is far from perfect, but it was written from the heart, in a kind of moment of enthusiasm. It forms a whole, and it would be difficult for me to add to it, subtract from it, or modify anything about it. I have tried to speak simply, without using too many technical terms, following in this the advice of Marcus Aurelius: "The work of philosophy is simple and discreet. Let us not get carried away by the swollen puffiness of solemn affectation" (*Meditations* 9, 29).

I sincerely believe that our most urgent and difficult task today is, as Goethe said, to "learn to believe in simplicity."[5] Might it not be the case that the greatest lesson which the philosophers of Antiquity—and above all Plotinus—have to teach us is that philosophy is not the complicated, pretentious, and artificial construction of a learned system of discourse, but the transformation of perception and of life, which lends inexhaustible meaning to the formula—seemingly so banal—of the love of the Good?

Yet Hadot himself, in his teaching and writings, has been a pioneer in warning against the dangers of interpreting ancient texts anachronistically: taking an isolated phrase, for example, as being highly revelatory of Plotinus' mentality—or even of that of an entire epoch—whereas in fact it may have been a literary allusion or cliché, dictated more by the literary genre than by Plotinus' own "genius." If I have tried to point out, more often than did Hadot, the occasions where Plotinus is quoting, borrowing, paraphrasing, or alluding to Plato, it is in the hope of calling attention to the subtle interplay of traditionalism and originality that constituted Plotinus' greatness. Far from being an exception for his time—much less the last representative of the pure, rationalistic Greek spirit before it was submerged by a tide of "Oriental" superstitions, as has sometimes been claimed—Plotinus was, in this sense at least, supremely representative of his time. He lived and wrote in a highly literate atmosphere, where the slightest allusion was likely to call to mind masses of Platonic, poetic, and other texts, by virtue of powers of memory of which we today can scarcely conceive.

I would hope, then, that Hadot's work can be enjoyed on two levels: without the footnotes, by the general public, who will find a

5. Quoted by V. Jankélévitch, *Bergson,* Paris, 1931, p. 254.

vibrant, living presentation of a thinker who is still capable of speaking to our everyday wants and needs, and with the footnotes by those who are geared to the more academic approach and who may, I hope, find the additional information I have added to be of some interest.

Finally, I should like to dedicate this translation to my grandfather, Jack Stephens.

Abbreviations Used in References

References to the text of the *Enneads* are given in the following form:
V 1, 12, 3: V = number of the *Ennead;* 1 = number of the treatise in that *Ennead,* 12 = number of the chapter of this treatise, 3 = line of this chapter as printed in the majority of modern editions.

References to Porphyry's *Vita Plotini* (*Life of Plotinus*) are given in the following form: V. P. 1, 2 = *Life of Plotinus,* chapter 1, line 2, as printed in most modern editions.

Introduction

Reading Hadot Reading Plotinus

Pierre Hadot's *Plotinus or The Simplicity of Vision* is a masterpiece of philosophical interpretation. Its mastery is exhibited not only in its interpretation of Plotinus, but also in its presentation of a vision of philosophy exemplified in, but certainly not exhausted by, the teachings of Plotinus. Originally published in French in 1963, its translation into English coincides with the appearance of the first volumes of Hadot's new translation of and commentary on Plotinus' *Enneads*. The thirty intervening years have seen the publication of many of Hadot's fundamental essays on Plotinus, essays that have permanently altered our understanding of Plotinus. But the best introduction to Hadot's reading of Plotinus remains this short book, for it allows us to see the experience of philosophy as manifested in the writings of a thinker too often consigned to the footnotes of philosophy.

Plotinus or The Simplicity of Vision was written as part of a series of books collectively entitled The Search for the Absolute and which, in addition to Plotinus, contained "psychoportraits" of writers such as Pascal, Bernanos, Kafka, and Dostoyevsky. Hadot's book was intended to provide a spiritual biography of Plotinus—not an analysis of all of the details of Plotinus' system—and it is as a spiritual biography that it should be read. Acknowledging the historical and textual difficulties encountered in any attempt to trace a portrait of Plotinus (chapter 1), Hadot turns to the question of how we can speak of Plotinus' self or soul, of how we are to understand the self in Plotinus' thought (chapter 2). The trajectory of the Plotinian self is to raise itself to the level of divine Intellect, to participate in the presence of Spirit (chapter 3). But this presence, this Spirit, is itself founded in a beyond, in the Plotinian One or the Good, which manifests itself as love and grace (chapter 4). It is at the level of the Good or the One that the most intense mystical experience is located, an experience that is as central as it is exceptional in the philosophy of Plotinus. Hadot insists that we should not take these levels of reality—from matter to Soul to Spirit to the One—as metaphysical abstractions, but rather as exhibiting stages of ascent, of spiritual or inner transformation.

Here is how Hadot summarizes this spiritual progress, as expressed by Plotinus in terms taken from the Platonic tradition. Plotinus

situates himself and his experience within a hierarchy of realities which extends from the supreme level—God—to the opposite extreme: the level of matter. According to this doctrine, the human soul occupies an intermediate position between realities inferior to it—matter and the life of the body—and realities superior to it: purely intellectual life, characteristic of divine intelligence, and higher still, the pure existence of the Principle of all things. Within this framework, the experience Plotinus describes for us consists in a movement by which the soul lifts itself up to the level of divine intelligence, which creates all things and contains within itself, in the form of a spiritual world, all the eternal Ideas or immutable models of which the things of this world are nothing but images. Our text even seems to give us to understand that the soul, passing beyond all this, can fix itself in the Principle of all things. . . .

Each degree of reality, he argues, can only be explained with reference to its superior level: the unity of the body is explained by the unity of the soul which animates it; the life of the soul requires illumination by the life of higher Spirit; and finally, we cannot understand the life of the Spirit itself without the fecund simplicity of the absolute, divine Principle, which is, in a sense, its deepest intimacy.

The point that interests us here, however, is that all this traditional terminology is used to express an inner experience. All these levels of reality become levels of inner life, levels of the self. Here we come upon Plotinus' central intuition: the human self is *not* irrevocably separated from its eternal model, as the latter exists within divine Thought. The true self—the self in God—is within ourselves. During certain privileged experiences, which raise the level of our inner tension, we can identify ourselves with it. We then become this eternal self; we are moved by its unutterable beauty, and when we identify ourselves with this self, we identify ourselves with divine Thought itself, within which it is contained.

Such privileged experiences make us realize that we never cease, and have never ceased, to be in contact with our true selves. (26–27)

Since, according to Hadot, all these levels of reality become levels of inner life, levels of the self, Plotinus' metaphysics cannot be separated from his spiritual experience. His spiritual biography represents the itinerary of philosophy itself.

Mystical union, however, does not permanently abolish the distinctions among discontinuous levels of the self. Mystical experience is transitory (Porphyry having reported that Plotinus reached the summit of this experience only four times during the six years Porphyry was present in his school), and Plotinus' soul does not remain up above, but returns to the exigencies of everyday life. How then can we reconcile the fleeting states of divine union with our normal lives, the fact that "we must look after our bodies and other people, think rationally, make provisions for the future" (65)? Hadot shows that, for Plotinus, the practice of the virtues assures a connection between the ecstatic and the everyday (chapter 5). Plotinian virtue expresses itself in a particular style of life and in a relationship with others that consists of mildness or gentleness. The secret of Plotinian gentleness is to be found in a transformation of one's whole being, a practice of virtue and contemplation that makes one present to Spirit while not excluding presence to other people, the world, and even the body (chapter 6). As Hadot writes elsewhere, "Presence to the self can thus be identical with presence to others on the condition that one has reached a degree of inwardness sufficient for discovering that the self, the true self, is not situated in corporeal individuality but in the spiritual world, where all beings are within each other, where each is the whole and yet remains himself."[1] In his final chapter, Hadot sketches the solitude that preceded Plotinus' death, and his meditations on the problems of evil and death that appear in his last works. He concludes by taking up the issue of our distance and proximity to Plotinus, insisting that while we cannot slavishly repeat the spiritual itinerary described in the *Enneads,* we risk a genuine loss if we ignore the dimensions of human experience to which Plotinus is witness.[2]

1. Pierre Hadot, "Plotinus and Porphyry" in *Classical Mediterranean Spirituality. Egyptian, Greek, Roman.* Edited by A. H. Armstrong (New York: Crossroad, 1986, p. 233).

2. My description of the structure of *Plotinus or The Simplicity of Vision* is indebted to discussions and correspondence with Pierre Hadot.

Thus, although mystical experience, our union with Spirit and
the One, is a central element of Plotinus' thought, the ascent of the
soul radically transforms our everyday life, our life down below, our
relations to our self, to others, and to the world. Just as there is a
feeling of strangeness when we surpass our everyday lives to live a
transcendent experience, so there is a feeling of strangeness when
we redescend, since "we are never quite the same again" (65). Here
is how Hadot describes the necessity of our living this discontinuity:

For Plotinus, the great problem is to learn how to live our day-to-day life. We
must learn to live, after contemplation, in such a way that we are once again
prepared for contemplation. We must concentrate ourselves within, gathering ourselves together to the point that we can always be ready to receive the
divine presence, when it manifests itself again. We must detach ourselves
from life down here to such an extent that contemplation can become a continuous state. Nevertheless, we still have to learn how to put up with day-to-
day life; better still, we must learn to illuminate it with the clear light that
comes from contemplation. For this, in turn, a lot of work is required: interior purification, simplification, unification.

    This is the task of virtue, of the importance of which Plotinus, as he grew
older, became more and more aware. While the treatises of his youth and
maturity, though they do recommend the practice of virtue, are primarily
hymns to the beauty of the spiritual world and the intoxication of ecstasy,
the works he wrote near the end of his life are devoted almost exclusively to
ethical subjects.

    The experience of divine union remains at the center of his thought. But
from now on Plotinus concentrates on showing how virtue, born from this
union, transforms one's entire being and becomes substantial wisdom. Any
contemplation which had no effect on concrete life, and did not culminate
in rendering man similar to God through virtue, would remain foreign and
meaningless to us. . . .

    Such is the soul's itinerary. Lifted up as far as the One by the latter's lib-
eral, gracious motion, the soul is not able to maintain herself at the summit
of herself, and falls back down again. Once back in practical life, consciousness, and discursive thought, however, she rediscovers within herself, here
down below, virtue: that trace of God which makes her similar to God. By
the practice of the virtues, the soul can rise up once more to the Intellect; in
other words, to a purely spiritual life. Once she reaches this state of perfection, virtue becomes wisdom: a stable state from which the soul may once
again render herself ready for divine union. (65–66, 68)

One finds in Plotinus a contrast between the momentary experience of divine union and the lengthy spiritual preparation necessary for this experience: "Plotinian philosophical life thus consists in a long waiting, a patient preparation, interrupted by brief, but vivid ecstasies, during which the soul reaches its end and its goal."[3]

I have quoted these passages from Hadot at length because they brilliantly articulate the major concepts and stages of Plotinus' spiritual itinerary. Fundamental to this vision of philosophy is the way in which Plotinus invites or exhorts us "to a conversion of attention" (30), his goal being to "mold his disciples by means of spiritual exercises" (18). As Hadot has shown in detail, in antiquity philosophy was a style of life: "The philosopher was less a professor than a spiritual guide: he exhorted his charges to conversion, and then directed his new converts—often adults as well as young people—to the paths of wisdom. He was a spiritual adviser" (75–76).[4]

The idea of a conversion of attention, of a turning of our attention away from a preoccupation with sensible things and toward the spiritual world, which is "nothing other than the self at its deepest level" (25), is Plotinus' version of the ancient idea that "philosophy was essentially conversion, that is to say a return to the self, to its real essence, by a violent uprooting from the alienation of unconsciousness."[5] In his arguments against the Gnostics, Plotinus makes clear that he does not believe that sensible things are evil in themselves; rather it is the concern we have for such things that distracts our attention: "We allow ourselves to be absorbed by vain preoccupations and exaggerated worries . . . [It is this] *concern* . . . which prevents us from paying attention to the spiritual life which we unconsciously live" (31). If we wish to be conscious of those transcendent things already present in the summit of the soul, we must turn inward and orient our attention toward the transcendent. As Plotinus describes it in *Ennead* V, 1, 12, 15–21:

3. Pierre Hadot, "Histoire de la pensée hellénistique et romaine: Réflexions sur l'expérience mystique plotinienne" in *Annuaire du Collège de France, 1990–91: Résumé des cours et travaux* (Paris, 1992), p. 482.

4. See also Pierre Hadot, *Exercices spirituels et philosophie antique*, 2d edition revised and enlarged (Paris: Études Augustiniennes, 1987); and Ilsetraut Hadot, "The Spiritual Guide" in *Classical Mediterranean Spirituality. Egyptian, Greek, Roman.*

5. Pierre Hadot, *Exercices spirituels et philosophie antique*, p. 181.

It is as if someone were waiting to hear a long-desired voice; he turns away from all other sounds, and awakens his ear to the best of all audible things, lest it should happen by. It is the same for us in this world: we must leave behind all sensible hearing, unless it is unavoidable, and keep the soul's power of perception pure and ready to hear the voices from on high.[6]

We are not metaphysically divorced from our true self, since the transcendent is present within us, but we find ourselves spiritually distant from it, distracted, unconscious of the deepest level of our self. The reorientation of our attention requires an inner transformation, a metamorphosis of our whole being; there is not some other place to go to find ourselves, to rediscover the divine within us: "To find God, it is not necessary to go to the temples he is supposed to inhabit. We do not have to budge to attain his presence. Rather, we must ourselves become a living temple, in which the divine presence can manifest itself" (45). To become ourselves a living temple requires arduous effort and continuous concentration, the practice of spiritual exercises and moral purifications that cannot but radically transform our entire way of being. Philosophy, the philosophical life, must be unceasingly renewed; it is a constant quest of self-transformation whose spiritual culmination lies in the self's becoming divine Spirit or Intellect, and, even more rarely, in the self, united to Spirit, experiencing, coinciding with, the Good.

Plotinus' mysticism has exerted a profound fascination and influence on the history of Western thought. No one has done more than Pierre Hadot to describe and clarify the structure and content of this mysticism. Consonant with the Aristotelian tradition, Plotinus presents the identity of the soul with divine Spirit or Intellect as an experience that transcends the normal activity of reason, extinguishing our reflective, discursive consciousness. Being united to divine Spirit, the soul lives the life of Spirit. But Plotinus did not believe, as Aristotle did, that divine Spirit is the supreme reality; rather, Intellect undergoes a process of formation in which it emanates from the prior unity of the Good or One: the One is the "ground or ultimate source of spiritual life [because it] is pure, simple, unde-

---

6. Hadot discusses this passage at length in "Les niveaux de conscience dans les états mystiques selon Plotin," *Journal de psychologie,* nos. 2–3, 1980. See especially p. 251.

composable presence" (58). According to Plotinus, the divine Spirit has two kinds of relation with the Good that transcends it; one of these relations is properly described as an intellectual relation and the other as a mystical one (although, when entered into by us, both of them bring about a loss of our normal consciousness). These two relations correspond to two phases in the formation of Intellect. The properly intellectual relation corresponds to the phase of the completely finished Intellect in which the Intellect sees the Good mediated or refracted through the universe of Forms that it itself thinks. The mystical relation corresponds to the phase of Intellect as it is being born, as it arises from the One, when it is still indeterminate, not yet Intellect. In this state, Intellect is in an unmediated, nonintellectual contact with the Good, which is felt as a kind of drunkenness and loving union. Thus Plotinus' mysticism has two stages or levels: the soul must first transform itself, separating itself from discursive reasoning and sensible consciousness, purifying itself so that it becomes Intellect; then, reascending to the original state of Intellect, it will refind the original unity in which Intellect found itself when emanating from the transcendent One. At this summit, the mystical experience in which the soul experiences the Good is the same as the mystical experience in which Intellect nonintellectually unites with the Good. The soul can only reach the Good when united to Intellect, a metamorphosis that requires the arduous spiritual exercises already described. But our nonintellectual contact with the Good, even after having identified with Intellect, cannot be brought about at will. We must wait for this experience, not knowing with certainty if it will come about, while, nevertheless, ceaselessly preparing for it.[7]

Plotinus' understanding of mystical experience has, as is obvious enough, an intricate metaphysical foundation, but it also gives rise to very precise spiritual or existential consequences. Plotinus' spiritual orientation, although borrowing from Plato the theme of the ascent of the soul that takes as its point of departure a lived amorous

7. In this description of Plotinus' understanding of mysticism, I have closely followed Hadot, "Plotinus and Porphyry," "Histoire de la pensée hellénistique et romaine: Réflexions sur l'expérience mystique plotinienne," and "Histoire de la pensée hellénistique et romaine: Plotin et l'expérience mystique" in *Annuaire du Collège de France, 1983–4: Résumé des cours et travaux* (Paris, 1984).

experience, has a very different psychological tone and content from Plato's description in the *Symposium*. This is how Hadot contrasts the two related experiences:

> Experience always takes place within a given attitude and a given inner perspective. . . . Platonic love rises, through a series of intellectual operations, up to the contemplation of Beauty; Plotinian love, by contrast, waits for ecstasy, ceasing all activity, establishing the soul's faculties in complete repose, and forgetting everything, so as to be completely ready for the divine invasion. The soul's highest state is complete passivity, and she tries to maintain herself in this state. Platonic love, once it has reached Beauty, displays its fertility in multiple thoughts and actions, producing science, education, and the organization of the state. Plotinian love, by contrast, refuses to return to day-to-day activity. It redescends to the world only when forced to do so by the needs of the human condition. (56)

We must be careful not to ascribe the replacement of activity by passivity to Plotinus in his representations of our spiritual journey. It is not a question of activity and passivity being mutually exclusive in the soul's ascent to the Good. Plotinus insists that we must constantly exercise ourselves in order to prepare for the coming of the Good, that the soul must learn to "leave behind all inner activity, distinct representations, self-will, and individual possessions" if it is to unite with the Good, since the Good is absolutely simple, without form (57). But our activity is not sufficient for nonintellectual union with the Good; the highest point of mystical ecstasy is not wholly within our own means, not simply a matter of greater power or willfulness.

According to Hadot, the ultimate foundation of the life of divine Intellect is grace: life is grace because the Good is grace. Without wanting to Christianize Plotinus, Hadot points to that aspect of Plotinus' experience of mysticism that highlights the good fortune (*eutuchein*) of the soul's union with the Good, the fact that the coming of the Good appears suddenly and unexpectedly and we are as if carried away by a kind of wave.[8] Distinct from the specifically Christian concept of grace (but also from Plato's depiction of the loving

8. See, for example, Pierre Hadot, "Histoire de la pensée hellénistique et romaine: Réflexions sur l'expérience mystique plotinienne," p. 482, and "Plotinus and Porphyry," p. 248.

ascent of the soul as the "motor force for an intellectual, almost scientific process"), Hadot has us understand that for Plotinus "if *philosophical reflection* goes to its own extreme, and still more if it attempts to express the content of the mystical experience, it, too, will be led to this notion of gratuitousness" (54, 51; my emphasis). Thus, although it is only given to the soul which has prepared itself, which has made itself like the Good by stripping away all form, the presence of the Good still appears as a good fortune, a "gratuitous surplus" (50).[9] Hadot succinctly depicts the existential intertwining of activity and passivity in Plotinus' "invitation" to mystical experience when he writes that in describing a state of passivity, Plotinus "is inviting his readers to *bring about this passivity in themselves*" (57; my emphasis).

The historical and philosophical import of Plotinus' description of mystical union should not be detached from Plotinus' understanding of the self. His conception of levels of the self insures that the telos of the philosophical life will be everywhere reflected in how he represents the self, and in how he urges us to experience its presence. Our distance from Plotinus makes it all too easy for us to ignore his conception of the true self as surpassing our individuality, of the human self's being freed from every limitation in a dilation of itself in the All. Just as Hadot has argued that Michel Foucault's interpretation of Stoicism does not take account of the cosmic dimension, the dimension of cosmic consciousness, inherent in the Stoic ideal of wisdom, demonstrating that Foucault focuses too exclusively on the Stoic conversion to self while ignoring the ancient sage's attempt to surpass himself in order to situate himself at a universal level,[10] so we find an analogous problem in certain attempts to use Hadot's own interpretation of Plotinus' account of the self.

In his magnificent and widely discussed essay "Le mythe de Narcisse et son interprétation par Plotin," Hadot shows that, for Plotinus, Narcissus represents a failure of spiritual ascent, a compla-

9. See Pierre Hadot's commentary on *Ennead* VI, 7, 34, 1–38 in *Plotin. Traité 38, VI, 7, Introduction, traduction, commentaire et notes par Pierre Hadot* (Paris: Les Éditions du Cerf, 1988), especially pp. 336–39.

10. Pierre Hadot, "Réflexions sur la notion de 'culture de soi'" in *Michel Foucault: Philosophe* (Paris: Éditions du Seuil 1989); and Pierre Hadot, "Le sage et le monde" in *Le temps de la réflexion* 10 (1989), pp. 176–77.

cency that leads the soul to allow itself to be fascinated by its corporeal reflection, to fail to see that the reality of the body comes from
the soul, whose light animates the body. Narcissus is a symbol of
the poverty and wretchedness of those human beings who never go
beyond the beauty of the body, who are sunk in the "dark depths
hostile to Intellect." Against the Gnostics, Plotinus does not make
Narcissus a cosmological symbol, since he does not believe that the
sensible world originates as a result of some narcissistic defect. In
itself, the sensible world is a good thing, a universal and normal
phenomenon of nature. Narcissus represents a moral and spiritual
state, the result, after the constitution of the sensible world, of
what transpires when the soul *directs its attention toward the body.*[11]
To the figure of Narcissus, Plotinus opposes the figure of Ulysses,
whose flight consists in discovering, first, that the body is only the
reflection of a prior light which is the soul itself and to which we
must return; in the next stage, the soul recognizes that its own light
is also only the reflection of another light, which is that of Intellect
or Spirit; finally, Intellect appears to itself as the diffraction of the
light of the primordial One.[12] This flight of Ulysses, these stages
of conversion toward the light, correspond, for Plotinus, to a total
change in our mode of vision: we must exchange one way of seeing
for another, which, Plotinus says in *Ennead* I, 6, 8, 26, "everyone has
but few use."[13]

Some years ago, R. Harder, one of the best Plotinus scholars,
raising questions pertinent to this Plotinian opposition between
Narcissus and Ulysses, asked whether Ulysses was anything more
than an anti-Narcissus, an inverted Narcissus, and whether we
might not appropriately apply the term *autoerotic* to the Plotinian
ascent. Harder wondered whether Plotinus did not substitute for the
complacency that led the soul to allow itself to be fascinated by its
corporeal reflection another more subtle complacency, that of the

11. Pierre Hadot, "Le mythe de Narcisse et son interprétation par Plotin," *Nou-
velle revue de psychanalyse,* no. 13, (spring 1970). The quoted phrase, from *Ennead* I,
6, 8, 8, is discussed by Hadot on p. 99. The arguments against the Gnostics are discussed on pp. 100–102.

12. Hadot, "Le mythe de Narcisse," p. 103–4.

13. Hadot, "Le mythe de Narcisse," p. 104.

beautiful soul for itself.[14] Plotinus' texts do sometimes seem to displace the Platonic dialogue between master and disciple by an erotic monologue directed toward the self.[15] Would not the fascination of the beautiful soul for itself be another form of autoeroticism, a higher kind of autoeroticism than Narcissus' but an autoerotic self-complacency nonetheless? More recently, Julia Kristeva, in her influential book *Tales of Love*, without taking up the same scholarly details as Harder, focuses on Plotinus' interpretation of the myth of Narcissus while stressing "the originality of the narcissistic figure and the very particular place it occupies, in the history of Western subjectivity."[16] Kristeva insists on the application of the term *autoerotic* to Plotinus' thought, claiming that "one witnesses a masterful synthesis between the Platonic quest for ideal beauty and the autoeroticism of one's own image," that for "the narcissistic shadow, a snare and downfall," Plotinus "substitutes autoerotic reflection," even allowing himself to "rehabilitate the *activity* of the narcissistic process."[17] Thus she writes that "The *Enneads* close with an apology of solitude oriented toward the One, as by an assumption of narcissism."[18] She even goes so far as to speak of Plotinus' "autoerotic jouissance"[19] and of the "price . . . that is paid for this luminous, reflective closure of psychic, autoerotic space under the constituent eye of the One."[20] It is Plotinus, according to Kristeva, who is responsible for "causing Platonism to topple over into subjectivity."[21]

Ironically, Kristeva repeatedly invokes Hadot's essay on Plotinus'

14. Hadot discusses Harder's view in "Le mythe de Narcisse," p. 105. Harder's concerns are to be found in R. Harder, *Plotinus Schriften* (Hamburg: Meiner, 1956–71), vol. 1, p. 381. The text most specifically at issue is *Ennead*, I, 6, 9, also cited by Kristeva. I cite and discuss this text in what follows.

15. Pierre Hadot, "Le mythe de Narcisse," p. 105, mentions the relevant texts.

16. Julia Kristeva, *Tales of Love* (New York: Columbia University Press, 1987), p. 105.

17. The quotations are from Kristeva, *Tales of Love*, pp. 108–9.

18. Kristeva, *Tales of Love*, p. 114.

19. Kristeva, *Tales of Love*, p. 108.

20. Kristeva, *Tales of Love*, p. 117. The psychological judgments that Kristeva makes concerning Plotinus' character are precisely the kinds of judgments that Hadot warns against in chapters 1 and 6 of this book.

21. Kristeva, *Tales of Love*, p. 117.

interpretation of the myth of Narcissus in support of her claims. But Hadot cautions us to be careful not to be misled by Plotinus' talk of the self, that to apply the term *autoerotic* to his conception of the self can only lead to misunderstandings. We will misread the Plotinian ascent, if we think of Plotinus' self as his individual self taking refuge in itself. Plotinus' conceptions of spiritual progress and of the levels of the self require the self's ascent to be a surpassing of one's individuality, a raising of oneself beyond every kind of autoeroticism. Despite Kristeva's use of Hadot, Hadot's interpretation could not be further from hers, could not emphasize more forcefully the philosophical distinctiveness of Plotinus' understanding of the self, a distinctiveness that precisely prohibits any toppling over into subjectivity.

Here is the passage, long but extraordinary, in which Hadot shows us how Plotinus' conception of the self is incompatible with the charge of autoeroticism.

Indeed, one must understand well the reasons for which Plotinus is called to speak of the "self" and what the "self" means in this context. We have said that for him it is a question of provoking a reversal from the "narcissistic" tendency that makes the individual take an interest only in what he believes to be his self, that is, his own body. The essential point of this method therefore consists in making the soul discover that the "self" is other than the body. We have described above the stages of what one could call the flight of Ulysses. It is a question of reascending toward the principle from which the corporeal reflection emanates: this principle is recognized successively as soul, as Intellect, as primordial Unity. The exercise consists therefore in turning consciousness away from the attention to and exclusive concern with the body in order to return it inward, that is to say, at first, toward the "self" as a free and independent subject (as a pure soul). This coming to consciousness of the "self" is already an ethical movement, it is already a purification that brings the soul back to its pristine purity, to the state of form disengaged from matter. But if this purification is to be perfectly realized, this pure form also has to reveal itself as pure thought. This means that the self raises itself from the level of the soul to the level of the Intellect. In the whole description of this movement of conversion, Plotinus is quite compelled to situate himself in the perspective of the "self," since it is a question of dissolving a false "self," the corporeal reflection, in order to make a true "self" be born, the soul raised to the level of Intellect. But this true "self" transcends the common and usual notion of "self." The Intellect, for Plotinus, is nothing other than the thinking of the All. It is precisely in reaching this level that the "narcissistic" soul will be perfectly given up. Indeed, the soul passes from a vision that is partial, external, misleading, and anguished to a vision that is total, internal, true, and peaceful. To raise itself to the level of Intellect, of the thought of the All, is properly and precisely to surpass the limits of individuality, of that concern for the partial that brings on the state of narcissism of the soul. In the works of Plotinus, individuality and totality are radically opposed, they mutually repudiate one another: "In becoming 'someone,' one becomes not-All, one adds a negation to the 'All.' And this remains until one does away with this negation. If you set aside everything that is other than the All (that is to say, the naught of individuality), you become larger. If you set that aside, the All will be present to you." In arriving at the level of Intellect, the human "self" arrives at a universal and total vision of reality, in which every particular point of view must give way. Can one speak of the "self" at this level? That will only be possible if one understands by the "self" not individuality entrenched in itself, but the interiority of consciousness that, as soon as it apprehends itself as interiority, accedes to the universality of the thought of the All. There is therefore no aesthetic and erotic complacency for the "self" in the texts that we have cited above. "To see one's own beauty" does not mean: to see a beauty that pleases "me" because it is "my self," but to see in my "self," that is to say, thanks to my conversion toward interiority, the Beauty that is nothing other than the All in its noetic necessity. Arriving at these transcendent levels, the human "self" no longer knows if it is a "self."[22]

I know of no more powerful description of the Plotinian ascent, no clearer narration of the transformation of oneself required to go from a partial, anguished vision to a total, peaceful one. The soul's ascent does not culminate in an experience, an emotion, that has the individual self for its object; rather, it experiences a transcendent presence with which it sees itself becoming identical. At the summit of this ascent, there is not so much an experience of self as an experience of an Other than self, an experience of oneself becoming Other,

---

22. Hadot, "Le mythe de Narcisse," pp. 105–6. The internal quotation from Plotinus is from *Ennead*, VI, 5, 12, 22. I have translated Hadot's French translation of Plotinus as literally as I could in order to preserve the exact sense of his interpretation of this passage. Hadot also cites the passage in this book on p. 110, in conjunction with his discussion of the last words attributed to Plotinus.

that is, of uniting with the One.[23] That is why, at this level, the human self no longer knows if it is a self; its own most profound interiority is at the same time its own self-transcendence, its accession to a universality liberated from every limitation.

In *Ennead* I, 6, 9, Plotinus presents the figure of the sculptor and his statue:

Go back inside yourself and look: if you do not see yourself as beautiful, then do as a sculptor does with a statue he wants to make beautiful: he chisels away one part, and levels off another, makes one spot smooth and another clear, until he shows forth a beautiful face on the statue. Like him, remove what is superfluous, straighten what is crooked, clean up what is dark and make it bright, and never stop sculpting your own statue, until the godlike splendor of virtue shines forth to you. . . . If you 'have become this and seen it, and become pure and alone with yourself, with nothing now preventing you from becoming one in this way, and have nothing extraneous mixed within yourself, but wholly yourself, nothing but true light, not measured by dimensions, or bounded by shape into littleness, or expanded to size by unboundedness, but everywhere unmeasured, because greater than all measure and superior to all quantity; if you see that this is what you have become, then you have become vision. Be confident in yourself: you have already ascended here and now, and no longer need someone to show you the way. Open your eyes and see. This alone is the eye that sees the immense Beauty.[24]

When the soul sculpts its own statue, it does not aestheticize or eroticize itself, but goes through a process of purification, chiseling away, removing what is superfluous, taking away everything extraneous so that there is nothing inwardly mixed with the true self. Thus the self, now transfigured, will not be measured by dimensions, and, everywhere unmeasured, will have become godlike. In this way, abandoning all individual and particular contingencies, it will rise back up "to that which, within itself, is more itself than itself" (21). The peak of this ascent is linked to joy, but, far from being

23. Hadot, "Le mythe de Narcisse," p. 107. For more detailed discussion of these topics, see also chapter 4 of this book and "Les niveaux de conscience dans les états mystiques selon Plotin."

24. Hadot cites part of this passage on p. 21. In providing a fuller quotation, I have mainly used the translation of the *Enneads* by A. H. Armstrong in the Loeb Classical Library. See also *Exercises spirituels et philosophie antique,* pp. 48–49.

an autoerotic jouissance, it is an unspeakable joy so great, so heightened, that when possessed by it the self, its individuality overcome, remains indifferent to everything else, including even the suffering of the body.[25] It is the joy of a self beyond itself, of a self that has surpassed itself in ecstasy.

Pierre Hadot is well aware of the fact that the Plotinian journey of the soul is, as often as not, viewed suspiciously nowadays, as though the call to the mystical is a deceptive invitation to mystification. Warning us of the threat of mystification, of the possibility of allowing mysticism to lead to mystification, he also insists that Plotinus' lived experience was not a means of escape, not a way of evading life but of being absolutely present to it. If we ignore those dimensions of human experience that include the "mysterious, inexpressible, and transcendent" (113), we shall succumb to another kind of mystification, one that is "just as tragic, although more subtle" (112).

Hadot closes this book, perhaps surprisingly to some readers, by invoking Wittgenstein's remarks on the mystical. He has written that "the 'mystical' seems to correspond, for Wittgenstein, to an existential and lived plenitude that escapes all expression."[26] And he has also claimed that Wittgenstein's *Tractatus* is a spiritual exercise.[27] On Hadot's reading, "Knowledge, for Plotinus, is always experience, or rather it is an inner metamorphosis" (48). As Wittgenstein says in *Tractatus* 6.43: "The world of the happy man is a different one from that of the unhappy man." How can we effect a self-transformation that is experienced as the appearance of a different world, a new life? How can philosophy be a lived exercise? Hadot's presentation of Plotinus gives us the rigors of philosophy, but also its joys. I can think of no better way to gain access to this experience of philosophy than by reading Hadot reading Plotinus.

25. Pierre Hadot, "Histoire de la pensée hellénistique et romaine: Réflexions sur l'expérience mystique plotinienne," p. 484. See also p. 72.

26. Pierre Hadot, *Exercises spirituels et philosophie antique,* p. 192.

27. *Exercices spirituels et philosophie antique,* p. 10.

I

Portrait

Never stop sculpting your own statue.

(I 6, 9, 13)

What do we know about Plotinus? A few details, not very much in the last analysis. We possess a life of the philosopher, written by his disciple Porphyry in about 301 A.D. Porphyry piously preserved a few anecdotes, a few personality traits, and recollections of conversations with his master. But Plotinus never used to talk about what his life had been like before he came to Rome during the reign of the emperor Philip. He said nothing about his homeland, his ancestors, or his childhood. It was as if he refused to identify himself with the individual named "Plotinus"; as if he wanted to reduce his life to his thought. With such scanty information, how can we sketch a portrait of the soul of Plotinus?

Someone might object: "But there are his works. We have these fifty-four philosophical treatises, put together by Porphyry under the general—and artificial—title of the *Enneads*. Isn't it *there* that we'll find the soul of Plotinus?"

And yet a literary monument from antiquity is something very different from a modern composition. Nowadays, it is possible for an author to say, "I *am* Madame Bovary."[1] Today, authors lay themselves bare, expressing and liberating themselves. They strive for originality, for what has never been said before. Philosophers set forth their system, expounding it in their own personal way, freely choosing their starting point, the rhythm of their expositions, and the structure of their work. They try to stamp their own personal mark on everything they do. But like all productions of the last stages of antiquity, the *Enneads* are subject to servitudes of a wholly different nature. Here, originality is a defect, innovation is suspect, and fidelity to tradition, a duty: "Our doctrines are not novel, nor do they

1. [As did the great French novelist Gustave Flaubert (1821–80), with regard to the heroine of his most famous novel, *Madame Bovary.*—Trans.]

17

date from today: they were stated long ago, but not in an explicit way. Our present doctrines are explanations of those older ones, and they use Plato's own words to prove that they are ancient" (V 1, 8, 10–14).

Philosophy has become exegesis or preaching. As exegesis, it restricts itself to commenting on the texts of Plato or Aristotle. In particular, it attempts to reconcile texts, when they seem to present contradictions. It is in the course of these attempts at reconciliation and systematization that individual originality comes into play. As preaching, philosophy becomes an exhortation to a life of virtue; here again, it is guided by centuries-old themes and backdrops. The philosopher was a professor and a spiritual guide, whose goal was not to set forth his vision of the universe, but to mold his disciples by means of spiritual exercises. Thus, Plotinus' writings are above all either sermons or textual explanations; often, they are merely the transcripts of his public classes.

Opening these old books, then, the modern reader has to be extremely careful. We run the constant risk of mistaking a schoolroom commonplace for a revelatory detail. A psychoanalyst may think to have discovered a symptom where, in fact, there is only an impersonal banality. For example, one could follow the methods so dear to modern literary criticism, and approach Plotinus by studying the fundamental images which dominate his work: the circle, the tree, the dance. But most of these images are not spontaneous: they are traditional and imposed by the texts to be commented on or the themes to be developed. No doubt, we could specify the transformations Plotinus makes them undergo; the fact remains that they do not emanate from the depths of his personality.

In this case, then, literary history reveals itself to be an indispensable aid. Yet it is still not enough, because adding to our difficulties is the fact that Plotinus' immediate sources are almost totally unknown to us. We can, therefore, never be sure that a given doctrine genuinely belongs to Plotinus.

There is, indeed, one name in Plotinus' life. It is a great name, but unfortunately nothing more than a name: Ammonius. At the age of about thirty, when he was living in Alexandria, Plotinus went to hear Ammonius, on the advice of a friend. He cried out, "This is the man I've been looking for!" and remained as Ammonius' disciple for

eleven years. Ammonius always refused to write, so we can say next
to nothing about what his teaching might have been. We do know,
however, through Porphyry, that he had a very deep influence on
Plotinus.

When our philosopher arrived in Rome, he spent ten years without writing anything, and contented himself with giving lessons
"based on Ammonius' teachings" (V. P. 3, 33). Later, when he had
more fully worked out his own doctrines, his research was always
conducted "in the spirit of Ammonius" (V. P. 14, 15).

We know, moreover, also thanks to Porphyry, that some of
Plotinus' contemporaries reproached him with slavishly copying
Numenius, a Platonist philosopher who had lived a century earlier.
Most of Numenius' writings are lost, but it is true that some pages of
his which have been preserved are worthy of Plotinus.

In the midst of such uncertainties, will we be able to sketch a spiritual portrait of Plotinus? If we were dealing with an ordinary writer,
we would have to abandon our undertaking. How indeed can we
"psychologize" an author if we can never be precisely sure of what
does and does not belong to him?

Fortunately, the author in question is Plotinus. It is enough to
read a few of his pages to get the impression of a unique, incomparable, and irreplaceable tonality. The historian may note in passing:
"such-and-such an image is found already in Seneca or Epictetus,"
or "such-and-such a passage is repeated word for word in Numenius"; he is still swept along by an irresistible movement, which
he cannot analyze or reduce to a system of defined ideas. Conventional themes, texts requiring explanation, classic images, requirements of exposition: all this, finally, matters little. All is transfigured
by one fundamental but inexpressible experience: Plotinus has only
one thing to say, and in order to say it, he has recourse to all the
possibilities of the language of his time. And yet, he never will say it:

> Have we said enough now, and can we be released? But the soul is still in
> the pangs of labor, even more now than before. Perhaps it is now time for her
> to give birth, now that she has leapt upwards to him and been filled with
> birth pangs. No; we must sing another incantation, if we can find another
> one that works against the pain. Perhaps what we have already said would
> do, if someone were to chant it repeatedly. What novel kind of incantation
> could we find? For though the soul goes over all truths, even those in which

we participate, yet she still evades us if someone wishes her to speak and think discursively. In order for discursive thought to say something, it must consider its objects successively, for such is the unfolding of thought. Yet what kind of unfolding can there be, in the case of something which is absolutely simple? (V 3, 17, 15–25)

How else could we paint a portrait of Plotinus than by describing this infinite quest after the absolutely simple?

□

It is not certain that the portrait on the frontispiece of this book is authentic. This may perhaps disappoint our modern taste for historical exactitude and anecdotes, but the matter would no doubt have been indifferent to Plotinus himself. When one of his students asked his permission to have a portrait made of him, he refused outright. He gave the following explanation: "Isn't it enough that I have to bear this image with which Nature has covered us? Must I also consent to leaving behind me an image of that image—this one even longer-lasting—as if it were an image of something worth seeing?" (V. P. 1, 7–10).

To perpetuate the image of "an ordinary man," to represent an individual, is not art. The one thing worthy of detaining our attention, and of being fixed in an immortal work of art, can only be the beauty of an ideal form. If one is going to sculpt the figure of a man, let him gather together everything beautiful he can find. If you're going to make a statue of a god, says Plotinus, do as Pheidias did when he sculpted his Zeus: "He did not use any sensible model, but he took him as he would be, if Zeus wished to appear before our eyes" (V 8, 1, 38–40).

Art must not copy reality: in that case, it would only be an inferior copy of that copy which is the object perceived by our senses. The true function of art is "heuristic": through the work of art, we discover, or "invent,"[2] the eternal model, the Idea, of which sensible reality is a mere image. The work of art is an attempt to imitate this

2. [As in English, so the French word "inventer" derives from the Latin *invenire*, "to discover".—Trans.]

Idea. In this sense, the true portrait will attain to the true self: "Like as into Himself eternity at last changes him."[3]

Thus, the artist's work can be a symbol of the quest for our true self. Just as a sculptor tries, in a block of stone, to attain to the form which will render ideal Beauty perceptible, so must the soul seek to give herself spiritual form, by rejecting everything other then herself:

> Go back inside yourself and look: if you do not yet see yourself as beautiful, then do as the sculptor does with a statue he wants to make beautiful; he chisels away one part, and levels off another, makes one spot smooth and another clear, until he shows forth a beautiful face on the statue. Like him, remove what is superfluous, straighten what is crooked, clean up what is dark and make it bright, and never stop sculpting your own statue, until the godlike splendor of virtue shines forth to you. . . . If you have become this, and seen it, and become pure and alone with yourself, with nothing now preventing you from becoming one in this way, and have nothing extraneous mixed within your self . . . if you see that this is what you have become, then you have become vision. Be confident in yourself:[4] you have already ascended here and now, and no longer need someone to show you the way. Open your eyes and see. (I 6, 9, 7–24)

Bit by bit, the material sculpture conforms itself to the sculptor's vision. When, however, sculptor and statue are one—when they are both one and the same soul—soon the statue is nothing other than vision itself, and beauty is nothing more than a state of complete simplicity and pure light.

How could we paint the portrait of Plotinus without making our own this movement of purification, through which the self, separating itself from everything that is not truly itself, abandons the body, sense-consciousness, pleasures, pains, desires, fears, experiences, and suffering—in a word, all individual and contingent particularities—and rises back up to that which, within itself, is more itself than itself?

---

3. ["Tel qu'en lui-même enfin l'éternité le change," the famous first line of Mallarmé's *Tomb of Edgar Poe*. The translation is that of Wallace Fowlie, in *Mallarmé*, Chicago/London: Univ. of Chicago Press, 1953, p. 87 n.8.—Trans.]

4. [A Platonic reminiscence; cf. *Theaetetus* 148c: "Then have confidence in yourself and believe what Theodorus said about you." (H/T/B).—Trans.]

It is precisely this movement we shall find in Plotinus' works. His treatises are spiritual exercises in which the soul sculpts herself: that is, she purifies and simplifies herself, rises up to the plane of pure thought, and finally transcends herself in ecstasy.

The same truths we discovered in the case of the individual also hold with regard to the historical particularities of Plotinus' work. It hardly matters whether a given passage is Plotinus' own or not; what matters is that we rid ourselves of all "having" in order purely "to be."

Our ignorance of the life of Plotinus the individual and our uncertainties with regard to the works of Plotinus the individual correspond to the profound desire of the individual, "Plotinus." It is the only desire in which he would have recognized himself, and the only desire which defines him: no longer to be Plotinus; to lose himself in contemplation and in ecstasy: "Every soul is, and becomes, that which she contemplates" (IV 3, 8, 15–16).

Painting the portrait of Plotinus will thus be nothing other than disclosing, throughout his life and his work, the fundamental sentiments which, like the colors of a rainbow, compose the simple light of this one unique desire, this one attention perpetually straining towards the divine.

II

Levels of the Self

> But we . . . Who are we?
>
> (VI 4, 14, 16)

"Plotinus resembled someone ashamed of being in a body" (V.P. 1, 1). These are the words with which Porphyry begins his master's life story. Let us not be too hasty here to diagnose some morbid trait particular to our philosopher. If there is psychosis here, it is that of an entire age. The first three centuries of the Christian era witnessed a flourishing of Gnosticism and mystery religions. Man felt himself to be a stranger in this lower world, as if he had been banished into his body and the sensible world. The popularization of Platonism was, in part, responsible for this collective mentality: the body was considered a tomb and a prison; the soul was to separate herself from it because she was akin to the eternal Ideas; our true self was held to be purely spiritual. Astral theologies, too, must be taken into account: according to these, the soul is of celestial origin, and has come down here via a stellar voyage, during the course of which she has become encased in ever-thicker envelopes, the last of which is the terrestrial body.

This age was disgusted by the body.[1] This, moreover, was one of the reasons for pagan hostility towards the mystery of the Incarnation. As Porphyry put it clearly: "How can we admit that the divine became an embryo, and that after its birth, it was wrapped up in swaddling clothes, covered with blood, bile, and even worse things?"[2]

The Christians themselves, however, would soon realize that

1. I am now much less sure of about the existence of such a collective mentality. On the difficulty of applying the notion of "collective mentality," cf. the summary of my course given at the Collège de France in *Annuaire du Collège de France,* 1983–84, pp. 505–10 [Author's note of 1989].

2. Porphyry, *Against the Christians,* frag. 77, [ed. A. von Harnack, *Porphyrios gegen die Christen* (= Abhandlungen der Königlich Preussischen Akademie der Wissenschaften, Philosophisch-historische Klasse I), Berlin: Reimer, 1916—Trans.].

such arguments could be turned against anyone who, like the Plato-
nists, believed in the pre-existence of souls in a superior world: "If,
as the story goes, the souls were the Lord's offspring . . . they would
always dwell in the court of the King, and never would have left such
a blessed place. . . . They would never have rashly sought out these
terrestrial parts where they inhabit opaque bodies, intimately mixed
with blood and humors, in sacks of excrement and unspeakable pots
of urine!"[3]

One could say that every philosophy of this period tried to
explain the presence of this divine soul in a terrestrial body. Each
was responding to the anxious interrogation of men who felt like
strangers in this lower world: "Who were we? What have we become? Where were we? Into what have we been hurled? Where are
we going? Whence can liberation come to us?"[4]

Within Plotinus' school itself, some people answered this Gnostic
question with the reply particular to Gnosticism. For the Gnostics,
souls had fallen into the sensible universe as a result of a drama beyond their control. An evil Power had created the sensible universe,
and souls were imprisoned in it against their will, even though they
were particles of the spiritual world. Still, since they came from the
spiritual world, they still retained their spiritual nature. Their misfortune resulted only from the place in which they happened to be.
At the end of the world, when the evil Power would be defeated, their
ordeal would be over. They would return to the "Pleroma," or spiritual world. Salvation thus came from *outside* the soul, and consisted
in a change of place. It was dependent on the struggle between superior Powers.

□

Plotinus reacted passionately, in his classes and in his writings,
against this doctrine, which, decking itself out in a Platonic appear-

3. Arnobius, *Against the Pagans* II, 37 [cf. Arnobius of Sicca, *The Case against the
Pagans,* newly translated and annotated by George E. McCracken (= Ancient Christian Writers no. 7), 2 vols., New York: Newman Press, 1949—Trans.].

4. Clement of Alexandria, *Extracts from Theodotus* 78, 2. [cf. *The Excerpta ex The-
odoto of Clement of Alexandria,* edited with translation, introduction, and notes by
R. P. Casey (= Studies and Documents I), London: Christophers, 1934, pp. 88–89—
Trans.].

ance, threatened to corrupt his disciples. Despite superficial re-
semblances, Plotinus' fundamental experience was diametrically
opposed to the Gnostic attitude.

Like the Gnostic, no doubt, Plotinus felt, at the very moment
when he was inside his body, that he was still identical with what he
was *before* he entered the body. His self—his *true* self—was not of
this world. But Plotinus did not have to wait for the end of the world
for his self, spiritual in its essence, to return to the spiritual world.
This spiritual world was not, for him, a supraterrestrial or supra-
cosmic place, from which he was separated by the vastnesses of celestial space. Neither was it an original state, irretrievably lost, to
which he could be brought back only through divine grace. Rather,
this spiritual world was nothing other than the self at its deepest
level. It could be reached immediately, by returning within oneself.

> Often I reawaken from my body to myself: I come to be outside other
> things, and inside myself. What an extraordinarily wonderful beauty I then
> see! It is then, above all, that I believe I belong to the greater portion. I then
> realize the best form of life; I become at one with the Divine, and I establish
> myself in it. Once I reach this supreme activity, I establish myself above ev-
> ery other spiritual entity. After this repose in the Divine, however, when I
> come back down from intuition into rational thought, then I wonder: How
> is it possible that I should come down now, and how was it ever possible that
> my soul has come to be within my body, even though she is the kind of being
> that she has just revealed herself to be, when she appeared as she is in her-
> self, although she is still within a body? (IV 8, 1, 1–11)

This is the only explicitly autobiographical passage in Plotinus'
writings,[5] and in it we can definitely recognize the philosopher's
fundamental experience. Here Plotinus is alluding not to a continuous state, but to privileged moments. There occurs a kind of awak-

---

5. In his sermon *On Isaac or the Soul* IV, 1 [= Corpus Scriptorum Ecclesiastorum,
vol. 32, Vienna, 1897, pp. 650, 15,—651, 7; English translation by M. P. McHugh (=
Fathers of the Church no. 65), Washington: Paulist Press, 1965, pp. 10–65—Trans.],
St. Ambrose compares Plotinus' ecstasy with the ecstasy of St. Paul (2 Cor. 12:1–4):
"A blessed soul it is which penetrates the secrets of the Word. For, *awakening from the
body, becoming a stranger to everything else,* she seeks *within herself,* and searches, so
as to find out whether she can, in some way, reach divine being. When she is finally
able to seize it, *going beyond all other spiritual reality, she establishes her dwelling in it*
and takes her nourishment from it. So it was with Paul, who knew that he had been

ening: something which has, up until now, remained unconscious, invades the field of consciousness. Better still: the individual finds himself in a state he ordinarily does not experience; he engages in an activity beyond his habitual modes of consciousness and ratiocination. After these brief, fleeting flashes, however, he is utterly astonished to find himself, once more, as he was before: living inside his body, conscious of himself, reasoning and reflecting on what has happened to him.

Plotinus expresses his inner experience in terms consonant with the Platonic tradition. He situates himself and his experience within a hierarchy of realities which extends from the supreme level—God—to the opposite extreme: the level of matter. According to this doctrine, the human soul occupies an intermediate position between realities inferior to it—matter and the life of the body—and realities superior to it: purely intellectual life, characteristic of divine intelligence, and, higher still, the pure existence of the Principle of all things. Within this framework, the experience Plotinus describes for us consists in a movement by which the soul lifts herself up to the level of divine intelligence, which creates all things and contains within itself, in the form of a spiritual world, all the eternal Ideas or immutable models of which the things of this world are nothing but images. Our text even seems to give us to understand that the soul, passing beyond all this, can fix herself in the Principle of all things.[6]

---

transported into paradise; but did not know whether he had been transported in his body or outside of his body. For his soul *had awakened from his body*, and had departed, and risen up away from sensations and the bonds of the flesh, and having thus become a stranger to himself, he received into himself ineffable words which he understood but could not divulge, for, as he remarks, mankind is not permitted to speak of these things." What struck St. Ambrose was that, on the one hand, St. Paul said that he did not know whether he had been transported in his body or outside of his body, and that, on the other hand, Plotinus spoke of an awakening from the body. He therefore did not hesitate to describe St. Paul's ecstasy in terms borrowed from the ecstasy of Plotinus.

6. I now think that the text of IV, 8, 1, 1ff. alludes only to an elevation within the spiritual world considered as a whole, but does not contain any reference to an elevation going as far as the One, principle of all things. Cf. P. Hadot, "L'union de l'âme avec l'intellect divin dans l'expérience mystique plotinienne," in *Proclus et son influence: Actes du Colloque de Neuchâtel,* Neuchâtel: Editions du Grand Midi, 1986, p. 14.

Elsewhere, Plotinus rationally demonstrates the existence of this hierarchy, which was taken for granted within the Platonic tradition.

Each degree of reality, he argues, can only be explained with reference to its superior level: the unity of the body is explained by the unity of the soul which animates it; the life of the soul requires illumination by the life of higher Spirit; and finally, we cannot understand the life of the Spirit itself without the fecund simplicity of the absolute, divine Principle, which is, in a sense, its deepest intimacy.

The point that interests us here, however, is that all this traditional terminology is used to express an inner experience. All these levels of reality become levels of inner life, levels of the self. Here we come upon Plotinus' central intuition: the human self is *not* irrevocably separated from its eternal model, as the latter exists within divine Thought. This true self—this self in God—is within ourselves. During certain privileged experiences, which raise the level of our inner tension, we can identify ourselves with it. We then become this eternal self; we are moved by its unutterable beauty, and when we identify ourselves with this self, we identify ourselves with divine Thought[7] itself, within which it is contained.

Such privileged experiences make us realize that we never cease, and have never ceased, to be in contact with our true selves. We are always in God: "If we must dare, contrary to the opinions of others, clearly to state what seems to us to be the case, then it is as follows: even our [particular] soul has not come down entirely, but something of it always remains within the Intelligible world" (IV 8, 8, 1–3). If this is the case, everything is within us, and we are within all things. Our "self" extends from God to matter, since we are up above at the same time as we are down here on earth.

As Plotinus puts it, taking up an expression from Homer,[8] "our head strikes the heavens" (IV 3, 12, 5). Suddenly, however, a doubt arises: "How is it that, having such great things within us, we do not perceive them, but usually leave our powers inactive, even though they are so great? How is it that some people never activate them at

7. ["Divine thought," "the spiritual world," "the other world," "the Inteligible world," "the World of Forms", "the world up above," "Intellect," and "Spirit" are all equivalent terms in Neoplatonic thought. They designate the second Hypostasis of reality, consisting of all Platonic Forms or Ideas.—Trans.]

8. Homer, *Iliad* 4, 443. The concept is Platonic; cf. *Timaeus* 90a.

all?" (V 1, 12, 1–3). Plotinus' reply is immediate: "Not everything in the soul is immediately perceptible; rather, it comes through to "us" when it reaches perception. Yet as long as a part of our soul is active but does not communicate [this fact] to the perceptual apparatus, then the activity does not reach the entire soul" (V 1, 12, 5–8). Although it is part—the highest part—of our soul, we are thus not conscious of this higher level of ourselves. This higher level is our "self" within divine Thought, or rather, it is the divine thought of our "self."[9]

Can we really say that we *are* something of which we are not conscious? How, moreover, can we explain this unconsciousness?

> But we . . . Who are "we"? Are "we" only the Spirit,[10] or are we those who have added themselves on to the Spirit, and who came into being within time? We were other people before our birth, in that other world. . . . As pure souls, we were Spirit . . . we were a part of the spiritual world, neither circumscribed nor cut off from it. Even now, we are still not cut off from it. Now, however, another person, who wanted to exist and who has found us . . . has added himself on to the original person. . . . He joined himself on to the person we were then. . . . Then we became both: now we are no longer only the one we were, and at times, when the spiritual person is idle and in a certain sense stops being present, we are only the person we have added on to ourselves. (VI 4, 14, 16–31)

9. [The true self, like all intelligible entities, is located within the hypostasis of divine Thought/Spirit/Intelligence; cf. *Ennead* V 5 (32): "That the Intelligibles are not outside the Intellect." In a whole current of Platonic thought, moreover, the Intelligibles were conceived of as the thoughts of God; thus our true, intelligible self can be considered as one of the thoughts of God. Finally, our true self—which Plontius often refers to as "the inner man," or "our true 'us'"—is, although normally unconscious, the highest part of our soul, while at the same time it is identical with the hypostasis divine Thought/Spirit/Intelligence (see following note).—Trans.]

10. I have usually translated the Greek word *nous* by "Spirit," and the Greek word *noêtos* by "spiritual." French translators, first and foremost Emile Bréhier, usually translate these two words by "Intelligence" and "intelligible" respectively. I have resigned myself to using the words "Spirit" and "spiritual" (German translators often use "Geist" and "geistig"), in order to express, as far as possible, the mystical and intuitive character of Plotinian Intelligence. On this subject, cf. A.-J. Festugière, *Personal Religion among the Greeks* (= Sather Lectures vol. 26), Berkeley: Univ. of California Press, 1954, p. 45.

Consciousness is a point of view, a center of perspective.[11] For us, our "self" coincides with that point from which a perspective is opened up for us, be it onto the world or onto our souls. In other words, in order for a psychic activity to be "ours," it must be conscious. Consciousness, then—and along with it our "self"—is situated, like a median or an intermediate center, between two zones of darkness, stretching above and below it: on the one hand, the silent, unconscious life of our "self" in God; on the other, the silent and unconscious life of the body. By means of our reason, we can discover the existence of these upper and lower levels. But we will not *be* what we really *are,* until we become aware of these levels. If we could become conscious of the life of the Spirit, and perceive the pulsations of this eternal life within us, in the same way that we can, by paying close attention, perceive the pulsations of our physical heart, then the life of the Spirit would invade the field of our consciousness. Then this life would truly become "ourselves," and would truly be *our* life:

When the influences from above[12] do not act upon us, they are active in the direction of the upper world. They act upon us when they reach as far as the middle. What? Does not what we call "us" also include what comes before the middle? To be sure, but we must become conscious of this fact. It is

11. [The French word *perspective,* like its English equivalent, can mean not only "the art or science of representing natural objects as they appear to the eye" (Webster's New Collegiate Dictionary, 1953, s.v. "perspective" 2); but also "the appearance presented by visible objects" (*Oxford English Dictionary* 1971, s.v. "perspective" II 3 b); or "a visible scene, view or prospect . . . a vista" (ibid., II 5a) as well as "the relation or proportion in which the parts of a subject are viewed by the mind; the aspect of a matter or object of thought, as perceived from a particular mental 'point of view'" (ibid., II 3 d); "a mental view, outlook or prospect" (ibid., II 5 b); and especially the obsolete sense of "the action of looking into something . . . the faculty of seeing into a thing; insight, penetrativeness" (ibid., III, 7). This last sense is closest to the word's etymological derivation (the Latin *perspicere* meant "to look at closely," while "*perspicax,*" the adjective derived from it, meant "sharp-sighted"; cf. *The Oxford Dictionary of English Etymology,* Oxford 1966, s.v. All these meanings are active in Hadot's usage, and perhaps the least inadequate English translation of "centre de perspective" would be "point from which one may see clearly into things, thereby discovering their innermost nature."—Trans.]

12. [That is, the creative, formative emanations from the hypostases higher than those of the soul and of the sensible world.—Trans.]

not the case that we always use all that we possess, but only when we direct the middle part either upwards or in the opposite direction, or when we bring that which was in a state of potentiality or habitude into actuality.[13] (I, 1, 11, 2–8)

Plotinus, thus, invites us to a conversion of attention which, for him, is already identical with what Malebranche would later speak of as "natural prayer" (prière naturelle). The method is seemingly simple: "We must not look, but must, as it were, close our eyes and exchange our faculty of vision for another. We must awaken this faculty which everyone possesses, but few people ever use" (I 6, 8, 25–27). This process is all the more simple in that consciousness, in the last analysis, is a kind of mirror: it need only be polished and turned in a certain direction for it to reflect the objects that present themselves to it. We must therefore place ourselves in an inner disposition of calm restfulness, in order to perceive the life of Thought:

It seems that perception exists and occurs when the act of thought is refracted, and that which is active with relation to the life of the soul is, as it were, sent back, as happens with the image in a mirror, when its smooth, bright surface is undisturbed. In the latter case, the image occurs whenever the mirror is present, but when it is not present, or is not in the state we have described [then there is no image, but] that of which there could be an image is not any the less actually present. The same holds true in the case of the soul: when that within us which corresponds to the mirror, in which the images of discursive thought and of the Spirit are displayed, is undisturbed, then they are seen in it, and known, as it were, in a perceptual way. It is then that we first realize that Spirit and discursive thought are active. When, however, the mirror within us is broken, owing to the fact that the harmony of the body is disturbed, then Spirit and discursive thought continue their activity without any image. (I 4, 10, 6–18)

Here, Plotinus has in mind the limit-case represented by madness. The spiritual life of the sage will not be interrupted just because he loses consciousness of his spiritual life, or the mirror of his consciousness is broken by physical disturbances. Nevertheless, we

13. [Dunamis, hexix, energeia. Technical terms of Aristotelian psychology. Dunamis designates potentiality, an action capable of being exercised; hexis, the permanent disposition to act in a given way; and energeia, the actual exercise of the activity. Cf. Aristotle, On the Soul, 2, 5.—Trans.]

must try to understand why it is that we usually do not perceive the life of the Spirit within us. The reason is that our inner mirror—our consciousness—has become foggy and tarnished by our concern for terrestrial and corporeal things.

It is not life within the body which prevents us from being aware of our spiritual life; the former is, as such, unconscious. Rather, it is the *concern* we have for our bodies. *This* is the true fall of the soul. We allow ourselves to be absorbed by vain preoccupations and exaggerated worries:

> If there is to be perception of these great faculties within the soul, we must direct the faculty of sensation inwards, and make it concentrate its attention there. It is as if someone were waiting to hear a long-desired voice; he turns away from all other sounds, and awakens his ear to the best of all audible things, lest it should happen by. It is the same for us in this world: we must leave behind all sensible hearing, unless it is unavoidable, and keep the soul's power of perception pure and ready to hear the voices from on high. (V 1, 12, 12–21)

It is not out of hatred and disgust for the body that we must detach ourselves from sensible things. The latter are not, in themselves, evil. It is the *concern* they cause us which prevents us from paying attention to the spiritual life which we unconsciously live. Plotinus wants us to have, here and now, the same attitude towards concern about earthly things, and even the memory of these things, as the soul will have after death, when she rises up to the higher world:

> The more she hastens towards the upper regions, the greater is her forgetfulness, unless by chance her whole terrestrial life has been such that her memories are only of greater things. Indeed, even in this world, it is good "to be a stranger to human concerns";[14] necessarily, then, we must also avoid remembrances. Thus, if someone were to say that the good soul is forgetful, in this sense he would be right: the soul flees from multiplicity, and gathers the many together into one, and abandons the infinite. Thus she is not encumbered by multiplicity, but she is light and by herself. In this world, too, whenever she wishes, even while still in this one, to be in the other world, she abandons everything alien to her. (IV 3, 32, 13–22)

14. [Plato, *Phaedrus* 249c–d.—Trans.]

Is it, then, enough to give up worrying, and turn our attention towards the summit of our soul, for us to become immediately aware of our true life and our true self? Is this enough for us to have—at will, as it were—the privileged experiences Plotinus describes?

No. This is still only a preparatory, although indispensable, phase. It is just for a few, fleeting moments that we can identify ourselves with our true self, for the spiritual life which our true self constantly lives represents a higher level of tension and concentration than what is appropriate for our consciousness. Even if we raise ourselves up to this level, we won't be able to maintain ourselves there. And if we do attain it, it is not so much that we become aware of our higher self as that we *lose* awareness of our lower self. After all, our consciousness is only an inner sensation: it requires us to split into two, for there must be a temporal distance—however infinitesimal—between that which sees and that which is seen. Consciousness is thus more of a memory than a presence. It is inexorably tangled up in time. All it can give us is images, which it tries to fixate by expressing them in language.

By contrast, the activity of our real self takes place in total presence, eternity and perfect simplicity:

> We should remember that, even in this world, when we contemplate—and especially when we contemplate with extreme clarity—we do not turn towards ourselves intellectually. Rather, we possess ourselves, but our activity is directed towards the object, and we *become* the object . . . then we are only potentially ourselves. (IV 4, 2, 3–8)

Here we have the whole paradox of the human self: we only *are* that of which we are aware, and yet we are aware of having been more fully *ourselves* precisely in those moments when, raising ourselves to a higher level of inner simplicity, we lose our self-awareness.

This is why, in the autobiographical extract we quoted above, Plotinus said that every time he regained consciousness after one of his ecstasies, and returned from intuition to reflection, he wondered how it was possible that he had come back down. How, after having experienced the unity of the Spirit, could he return to the divisive alienation of his conscious self?

When it passes from one inner level to another, the self always has the impression that it is losing itself. If it unifies itself and rises up to pure thought, the self is afraid it will lose its self-consciousness and no longer possess itself. If, however, it comes to live the divine life, it is afraid of regaining consciousness and losing itself by splitting into two. From all this it is evident that consciousness is not, any more than memory, the best of things. The more intense an activity is, the less it is conscious.

Even when we are awake, we can find a great many fine activities, meditations, and actions which are not accompanied by consciousness at the very moment when we are meditating or acting. A person who is reading, for example, is not necessarily aware that he is reading, especially if he is reading attentively. Likewise, a person who performs a courageous act is not aware, at the moment that he performs the act, that he is acting courageously. (I 4, 10, 21–27)

In a sense, consciousness makes its appearance when there is a break in a normal state: illness, for instance, brings about a shock which causes us to become aware of it. If we are in good health, however, we are not aware of the state of our body. And that's not the worst of it: "Consciousness tends to render more faint those very activities which it accompanies. When they are alone [i.e., unaccompanied by consciousness], then they are pure; more active and alive. When even sages come to be in such a situation, their life is more intense, since it is not diffused in sense perception, but is gathered together in one place, within itself" (I 4, 10, 28–32).

Such states cannot, however, be prolonged. We are, irremediably, conscious beings, split into two. We want to seize these moments of unity, fixate them, and conserve them, but they escape us at the very moment when we think we have them, and we fall back from presence onto memory.

The only way, then, that we can raise ourselves up to spiritual life is by a kind of continuous oscillation between the discontinuous levels of our inner tension. We must, by directing our attention inside ourselves, prepare ourselves to experience the unity of Spirit, only to fall back down to the plane of consciousness, there to recognize that it is "we" who are "up above." Then, once more, we will lose awareness, to re-encounter our true self in God. More precisely, we must resign ourselves to the fact that we will retain only a confused self-consciousness during the moment of ecstasy: "It is a kind of understanding and perception of our Self, in which we must be very careful lest, wishing to perceive more, we do not stray away from our Self." (V 8, 11, 23–24).

Plotinus describes this oscillatory movement, which allows us to have the inner experience of our self in God—or of God within us— in the following terms:

> If we come to be at one with our self, and no longer split ourselves into two, we are simultaneously One and All, together with that God who is noiselessly present, and we stay with him as long as we are willing and able. If we should return to a state of duality, we remain next to him as long as we are pure; thus we can be in his presence again as before, if we turn to him again. Out of this temporary return to division, we have, moreover, gained the following benefit: in the beginning, we regain consciousness of ourselves, as long as we are other than God. When we then run back inside, we have everything [sc. consciousness *and* unity with God]. Then, abandoning perception out of fear of being different from God, we are at one in the other world. (V 8, 11, 4–12)

Plotinian inner experience thus reveals to us the existence of discontinuous levels of our spiritual life. Dispersed amongst the cares and preoccupations of daily life, we can, first of all, concentrate ourselves inwardly, direct our attention towards the things up above, and regain consciousness of ourselves. Then we shall discover that we can, at times, rise up to a more perfect inner unity, in which we attain to our living, real, veritable self within divine Thought. When we get to this level, perhaps we will touch a state of ineffable unity, in which we mysteriously coincide with the absolute simplicity out of which all life, thought, and consciousness proceed.

Yet these levels do not cancel each other out; rather, it is the interaction of all of them together which constitutes our inner life. Plotinus is not inviting us to the abolition of personality in *nirvana*. On the contrary, Plotinian experience reveals to us that our personal identity presupposes an ineffable Absolute, of which it is both the emanation and the expression.

III

Presence

If God were absent from the world, he would not be within you either.

(II 9, 16, 25)

Against the Gnostics, Plotinus affirmed that the spiritual world is not to be found elsewhere than within ourselves. Sometimes, to the vision of the purified soul, our transfigured self appears to itself as a "wonderfully majestic Beauty," and our inner life seems to be bathed in divine life. Plotinus was thus inviting us to a metamorphosis of our inner perception. As we saw above, consciousness must cease splitting itself into two, and come to coincide with our true Self, that higher level of tension and unity. We must learn to look within ourselves, in order to discover the spiritual world within us.

But if this is so, must we say that the sensible world is irreparably separated from this spiritual world? Are the Gnostics right to despise material nature, and see in it nothing but an artifact fabricated by an evil Power? No: although the spiritual world is within us, it is also outside us. Just as it was enough to learn to look within ourselves in order to discover this world, so it is enough to learn how to look outside ourselves in order to perceive the spiritual world behind the world of appearances. The metamorphosis of inner vision thus has as its counterpart the metamorphosis of physical vision.

The Gnostic does not know how to look at the world:

Who amongst these insanely conceited people is as well-ordered or wise as the All? . . . It is not for a wise person even to inquire about this, but rather for some blind person, having no perception or intelligence whatsoever, who, since he does not even look at this world, is far from being able to see the spiritual world. (II 9, 16, 32–39)

Those who look with the skilled eyes of an expert do not see the same things [as the uninitiate] when they look at paintings; rather, they recognize a sensible image of what was in the mind [sc. of the artist], and they are as if disturbed, and come to a recollection of the truth. It is from this experience that erotic desires are set in motion. One viewer, when he sees the beauty in

35

a well-portrayed face, is transported above. Another will have such a lazy mind that he is not moved towards anything else, but when he sees all the beauties of the sensible world, all its symmetry and great orderliness, and the form manifested in the stars, even though they are so far away, he is not seized by a feeling of awe, and he does not immediately think: "What wonders, and from what a source!" (II 9, 16, 43–55)

Knowing how to look at the world of the senses is to "prolong the vision of the eye by means of the vision of the spirit"; it is "to pierce the material envelope of things by a powerful effort of mental vision, and go on to read the formula, invisible to the naked eye, that their materiality makes manifest."[1] We might call this procedure "the Lynceus method," since the latter "could even see what is within the earth" (V 8, 4, 25).[2] It allows us to go beyond the material appearances of objects, and see their form:

Let us take this world, with each of its parts remaining what it is and not mixed up with one another, and imagine it in thought, insofar as is possible, as simultaneously One and All,[3] in such a way that, if one of the parts appeared, the presentation of the others would necessarily ensue. . . . For example, let us suppose that the sight of the sphere of fixed stars is necessarily followed by the presentation of the sun, and, at the same time, of the other stars. Let us imagine that we see the whole earth in this way, and the sea, and all living beings, as if in a transparent sphere, in which it really would be possible to see everything. Let us keep within our soul the luminous representation of this sphere, containing everything within itself. . . . Keep this image within yourself, and eliminate its mass; then eliminate the presentation you have within you of its spatial extension and its matter. (V 8, 9, 1–12; cf. II 9, 17, 4)

1. I have taken these expressions from H. Bergson, *La vie et l'oeuvre de Ravaisson,* in H. Bergson 1946, p. 258. As we shall see later, there is a great similarity between the philosophy of Ravaisson and the thought of Plotinus.

2. [In Greek mythology, Lynceus, son of Aphareus and twin brother of Idas, was lookout man for the Argonauts when they sailed in search of the Golden Fleece. He had such sharp eyesight he could see in the dark, or guess the location of buried treasure; cf. Homer *Odyssey* 11, 300; Apollodorus, *Library* III, 10, 3; 11,2.—Trans.]

3. [*Eis hen homou panta.* A pre-Socratic formulation. Anaxagoras (frag. 1 Diels-Kranz) used the term *homou panta* to describe the state of primal indifferentiation out of which the universe first arose, but Plotinus is more probably thinking of the earlier formulation by Parmenides, often quoted by the later Neoplatonists (frag. 8, 5–6 Diels-Kranz): "(Being) . . . is now altogether, one (*homou pan; hen*), indivisible . . ."—Trans.]

By this method, there appears before our eyes the world of Forms, which thus turns out to be the visible world freed from its materiality; that is to say, reduced to its Beauty: "From what source did the beauty of that Helen shine forth, over whom men fought so much, or of those women who rival Aphrodite in beauty? . . . Isn't it always a *Form* which moves us? . . . Beauty influences us once it comes to be inside us, but it comes in through the eyes as Form alone"[4] (V 8, 2, 9–26).

The emotion produced in us by visible beauty is thus caused by the Form made manifest in a body. The world of Forms is able to move us sensuously, and it is perceived with a pleasure that perceptible reality could never arouse:

There [sc. in the intelligible world], all things are filled, and, as it were, boiling over with life. It is as though they flowed like a stream, from one source—not from one breath or warmth.[5] Rather, it is as though there were one quality, containing within itself and preserving all the other qualities: that of sweetness along with fragrance; the quality of wine along with the powers of every juice, with visions of colors, and with all that is known by the sense of touch. Let there also be all that the ear can hear; each melody and every rhythm. (VI 7, 12, 22–30)

In this universe of pure Forms, where each Form is nothing other than itself, there is complete interpenetration:

All things are transparent, and there is nothing dark or resistant, but each Form is clear for all others right down to its innermost parts, for light is clear to light. Indeed, each has everything within it, and again sees all things in any other, so that all things are everywhere, everything is everything, each individual is all things, and the splendor is without end (V 8, 4, 4–8). . . . [Beauty] shines brightly upon all things, and fills whomever arrives there, so that they too become beautiful. Likewise, people often climb to lofty places, where the earth is colored golden-brown,[6] and are filled with that color, and made similar to that upon which they are walking. In that other

---

4. [In accordance with the Aristotelian theory of perception; cf. *On the Soul*, 2, 12, 424a17ff. (H/T/B)—Trans.]

5. [A jab at the Stoics; cf. Zeno's definition of God as "warmed breath" (SVF I, 135; H/T/B).—Trans.]

6. [*Xanthon*. Greek color terms are notoriously hard to translate, and this one is no exception: Bouillet and Bréhier rendered it as "golden," H/T/B "brown," Armstrong "red-gold," Sleeman/Pollet "yellow, brown." At any rate, the gist of the image

world, however, the color which blooms on the surface is beauty itself; or rather, each thing is color and beauty, right from its very depths. (V 8, 10, 26–30)

What, then, is the relationship between the visible world and the world of Forms? If the latter can be seen through the former, and if the vision of the spirit can prolong the vision of the eye, it is because there is continuity between the two worlds: they are the same thing, at two different levels. Plotinus insists strongly on this continuity. "Our world," he writes, "is not separated from the spiritual world" (II 9, 16, 11).

Plotinus was vigorously opposed to the anthropomorphism of Plato's *Timaeus,* which had, moreover, been taken up by the Gnostic sects. For him, the visible world was not the work of a Creator who had fashioned it by reasoning and reflecting:

Since we concede that this world has its being and its qualities from elsewhere, are we to imagine that its creator thought it up by himself, as well as the fact that it ought to be placed in the center; then he thought up water, and that it ought to be placed on top of the earth; and then everything else in order as far as the heavens? He thought up the animals next, I suppose, and assigned specific forms to each one of them, just as they have today, and for each of them he thought up their guts on the inside and their limbs on the outside? And then, once each thing had been properly arranged within his mind, only then did he set about his task? Nonsense; in the first place, such a conception is impossible—whence would it have come to him, when he had not yet seen anything? Secondly, even if he had received it from someone else, he could not have put it into action, like craftsmen do now by using their hands or their instruments: hands and feet did not come into being until later! The only alternative is that everything existed elsewhere (sc. in the spiritual world), but since there was nothing in between them, there suddenly appeared, as it were, by virtue of their proximity to each other within Being, an image and icon of the spiritual world. . . . The point is that you can perfectly well explain why the earth is in the center, why it is round, and why the ecliptic slants the way it does. In the other world, however, it was not because things had to be thus and so that it was decided to make

is clear enough: the important contrast is between the *superficial* coloration that we encounter in the phenomenal world and the complete being-filled with a color or other quality which occurs in the intelligible world.—Trans.]

them so; rather, it is because things are the way they are that they are good.
(V 8, 7, 1–15; 36–40)

This concept is dear to Plotinus:

Consider the wonderfully variegated workmanship we find in any spe-
cies of animals, and what we observe even in the case of plants: the lovely
shapes of their fruits and even of their leaves; the way they blossom forth
with generous spontaneity; their delicacy and variety (III 2, 13, 22–25).
This arrangement is so much in conformity with the Spirit that it had no
need of rational planning, but it is such that, even if someone had the most
excellent capacities for rational planification, he would be astounded, since
rationality could not have come up with any other way to make it. (III 2, 14,
14, 1–4; cf. VI 2, 21, 34–41)

The Spirit's vision, prolonging and developing the vision of the
eye, allows us to glimpse, behind the material world, a world of
Forms. The material world is nothing other than the "visibility" of
these Forms, and is therefore to be explained by them. The Forms,
for their part, have no need to be explained; it is useless to seek their
cause or their goal. They are the causes of themselves, and are not
the way they are because they *had* to be that way, but it is because
they are what they are that they must be that way. If the Forms require no explanation, and contain within themselves their own jus-
tification, the reason is that they are living beings: "That which is
inert and lifeless has no *raison d'être* at all; but if it is a Form and
belongs to the Spirit, whence could it derive its *raison d'être* [sc. except from itself]? (VI, 7, 2, 19–21).

The world of Forms is animated by a single Life: a constant movement which engenders the different Forms. It is like a single organ-
ism, which finds its raison d'être within itself, and differentiates
itself into living parts. The Forms become complex and subdivide
from the original Plant to the different kinds of plants, and from the
original Animal to the various kinds of animals. Each Form develops
that which it implies: the Form "human" requires reason, but also
feet and fingers. The Form "horse" implies the horseshoe, while
other animal Forms imply horns or antlers (VI 7, 10, 1f.). Each
Form, that is to say, wills itself to be complete and perfect in its own
way, according to its own theme. The world of Forms does not carry

out a program or plan above and beyond itself; rather, one could say that it invents and posits itself. It is, as Uexkhüll said of living organisms, "a melody that sings itself."[7] It is an immediate wisdom, "which is not acquired by calculations, since it has always been present as a whole; because it lacks nothing, it does not need to be sought after (V 8, 4, 36–37). This wisdom is not constructed out of theorems; it is complete, and it is a unity. . . . It is enough for one to posit it as holding the first place: it does not derive from anything else, nor is it in anything else" (V 8, 5, 5–9).

So as to make comprehensible his intuition of the life of the Forms, Plotinus borrows the example of hieroglyphs: "In the case of those things which they, in their wisdom, wanted to designate, the Egyptian sages did not use written characters, literally representing arguments and premises and imitating meaningful sounds and utterances of axioms. Rather, they wrote in pictures, and engraved on their temples one picture corresponding to each reality. . . . Thus, each picture is a knowledge, wisdom . . . perceived all at once, and not discursive thought nor deliberation" (V 8, 6, 1–9). Hieroglyphs, as Plotinus conceives them, give a good idea of what it is to be an organic totality: each Form is itself "all at once," and it gives its meaning to itself immediately. Plotinus' Forms, one could say, are hieroglyphs which draw themselves.

Thus we find the Platonic theory of Ideas metamorphosed into an intuition of the mystery of Life. It could be objected that the world of Plotinian Forms is only the "inside" of the visible world, and that it cannot explain concrete, materialized life. True, Plotinus is only proposing a theory of spiritual morphogenesis; but perhaps it is also true that all life is Spirit. Be that as it may, he did have the incomparable merit of elaborating the concepts without which the constitution of a philosophy of Life is impossible. He dared, as Goethe said, "to believe in simplicity." Life, for him, is a formative, simple, and immediate activity, irreducible to all our analyses. It is a totality

7. [Jakob Johann Baron von Uexkhüll (1864–1944), German naturalist and precursor of environmentalism. In 1926, he founded at Hamburg the Institute for Environmental Research (Institut für Umweltforschung), and published many works on the philosophy of Nature.—Trans.]

present all at once, within itself; a Form which forms itself; an immediate knowledge which effortlessly attains perfection.

It is at the source of Plotinus' thought that modern philosophies of Life have sought their inspiration. What is Goethe's "original phenomenon" (*Urphänomen*)[8] other than Form as Plotinus conceives it? And was it not from his meditations on the philosophy of Plotinus that Bergson derived his conception of the Immediate (*l'Immédiat*), his critique of finalism, and his sense of "organic totalities" (*totalités organiques*)?[9]

The contemplation of the world of Forms is an essential moment in Plotinus' spiritual life. It has been said that "mysticism is the recognition of the pure fact," because "the pure fact is mystery."[10] The Plotinian Forms are just such pure facts. We must give up trying to seek their cause; they have their cause and their meaning within themselves. In this sense, we can say that, for Plotinus, the world of Forms is the object of a mystical experience.

In this aspect of Plotinus' thought, moreover, we find a critique of human reflection and reason analogous to the critique of reflection and consciousness that had been set in motion by the discovery of different levels of the self. In both cases, the simplicity of life escapes the grasp of reflection. Human consciousness, living, as it does, split into two, and occupied by calculations and projects, believes that nothing can be found until it has been searched for; that the only way to build is to put various pieces together; and that it is only by using means that one can obtain an end. Everywhere it acts, consciousness introduces something intermediate. Life, by contrast, which is able to find without searching, invents the whole before the parts, and is end and means at the same time—which, in a word, is immediate and simple—is incapable of being grasped by reflection. In order to reach it, just as in order to reach our pure self, we shall have to abandon reflection for contemplation.

8. [For Goethe the *Urphänomen* was an original or basic law of nature, in and through which the Godhead manifested itself, and which accounted for the plurality of individual phenomena. Cf. J. P. Eckermann, *Gespräche mit Goethe,* Dec. 16, 1828; Feb. 13, 1829; Sept. 14, 1830, etc.—Trans.]
9. On Bergson's philosophy of life, cf. V. Jankélévitch 1975.
10. Jankélévitch, ibid., p. 292.

The reason for this is that life itself, at every level, is contemplation—a violent, but highly Plotinian, paradox.

Nature itself, the source of life for bodies, is already contemplation:

> If she were asked why she creates, she would reply—if, that is, she were willing to listen to the questioner and to speak—"You should not have questioned me, but understood in silence, just as I myself keep silent, for I am not accustomed to talk. What is there to understand? That what comes into being is the object of my silent contemplation, and that the product of my contemplation comes into being in a natural way. I myself was born of such contemplation; this is why I have a natural love for contemplation. My contemplation engenders the product of my contemplation, just as geometers draw figures by contemplating.[11] I, however, do not draw anything, but I contemplate, and the lines of bodies come into existence, as if they were issuing forth from me." (III 8, 4, 1–10)

This speech by the personification of Nature explains how the sensible world visibly manifests the world of Forms. Nature has no hands or brush with which to fabricate organisms copying the Forms. If Nature does design these organisms, it must do so by an art which is immediate. It is like a painter for whom it would be enough to look at his model in order for the image of the latter to draw itself on the canvas. *Natura pictrix!*[12] Recently, Roger Caillois drew our attention to the spontaneous art of Nature which "paints" the wings of butterflies.[13] We may also think of the purely ostentatious character that certain biologists perceive in the structures of plants, in which decorative ornamentation plays a role of fundamental importance. Here, once again, Plotinus has come close to the mystery of Life.

Nature contemplates that which Soul allows it to glimpse of the world of Forms. But Soul itself contemplates the world of Forms, and what it communicates to Nature is only the natural result of this contemplation. No doubt, Soul often abandons this contemplation

11. [In Antiquity it was thought that, just as painters reproduce a visible model in their art, so geometers copy the intelligible model of figures within their minds. Cf. Plato, *Republic* 510c–3.—Trans.]

12. ["Nature the painter."—Trans.]

13. Roger Caillois, *Méduse et Cie*, Paris 1960.

for discursive reasoning, for investigation, and for action, but in the last analysis, it does so out of love for contemplation:

> When people are too weak for contemplation, they switch to action, which is a mere shadow of contemplation and of reason. Since, owing to the weakness of their souls, their faculty of contemplation is insufficient, they cannot grasp the object of their contemplation and be fulfilled by it. Yet they still want to see it; and so they switch to action, in order to see with their eyes what they could not see with their spirit. In any case, when they create something, it is because they themselves want to see it and to contemplate it; and when they propose to act, insofar as they are able, it is because they want their act to be perceived by others. (III 8, 4, 33–39)

Thus, it is through contemplation that we can possess immediately what people can usually obtain by a lengthy detour: the vision of Beauty.

This Beauty is that of the world of Forms, where contemplation is immediate, and the Forms contemplate themselves. In them, the immediate art we glimpsed in Nature is brought to its ideal perfection: the Forms form themselves by contemplating themselves, and they posit themselves as they contemplate themselves. They are, at the same time, the model and result of themselves, in one single spiritual act. One single life and thought courses through them; they are one single Form which contemplates itself. They are divine Thought; that "Beauty itself" of which Diotima spoke in Plato's *Symposium*.[14] They are the Intellect: "The Intellect is beautiful; indeed it is the most beautiful of all things. Situated in pure light and pure radiance,[15] it includes within itself the nature of all beings. This beautiful world of ours is but a shadow and an image of its beauty. . . . It lives a blessed life, and whoever were to see it, and— as is fitting—submerge himself within it, and become One with it, would be seized by awe" (III 8, 11, 26–33).

In order to unite herself to divine Thought, in the midst of which the Forms contemplate themselves, the soul must cease contemplat-

14. [Cf. Plato, *Symposium* 211e.—Trans.]
15. [Cf. Plato, *Phaedrus* 250c: the glorious passage where the visions of the soul prior to incarnation are described in terms borrowed from the Eleusinian Mysteries.—Trans.]

ing this world of Forms as if it were something exterior. She must
experience this world within herself, by raising herself to the level of
pure contemplation characteristic of divine Thought. She must coincide at the very summit of herself, with this immediate vision of
herself: "If one were to compare [the world of Forms] to a living,
variegated sphere, or to something made up only of faces, shining
with living faces . . . then one would see it, but as it were from the
outside, as one being sees another; in fact, however, one must oneself become Spirit, and oneself become vision" (VI 7, 15, 24–32).

At this point, there is no longer any distinction between outer
and inner perception. We have gone beyond the level of reflection
and perception, and reached that of intuition and contemplation.
We now sense that Life is immediate self-contemplation, and we see
all things being born from this total vision, by means of which the
Beautiful appears to itself as vision. We "are" within the divine Intellect, the Thought which thinks itself:

> When [the Intellect] sees being, it sees itself; when it sees, it is in a state
> of actuality, and its actuality is identical with itself, since Intellect and the
> process of intellection are one and the same. It does not see one part of itself
> with another part of itself, but all of itself by means of the totality of it-
> self. . . . As long as we were up above, in the nature of the Intellect, we were
> satisfied: we thought, and, having gathered all things together into one, we
> contemplated. It was the Intellect which thought and spoke about itself,
> while the soul kept quiet and acquiesced in the action of the Intellect. Now
> that we have come to be in this world again, we would like the soul to be
> persuaded, too, as if we wanted to observe the model within its image. (V 3,
> 6, 5–8; 12–18)

As a result of this experience, we shall come to know that, since
all things result immediately from Beauty, the latter is just as much
present in the sensible world as it is in our soul. To the Gnostics who
despise the world, Plotinus can object: "God is present to all beings,
and he is in this world, however we may conceive of this presence;
therefore the world participates in God. Or, if God is absent from the
world, he is also absent from you, and you can say nothing either
about Him or the beings which come after Him" (II 9, 16, 24–27). As
long as we are in contract with the divine presence, there is no
longer any opposition between outer and inner world. It is the same
world of Forms, the same divine Thought, the same Beauty, where

all things commune in one single spiritual life, which we discover both within us and outside of us.

Porphyry tells us that Amelius, one of Plotinus' disciples, was extremely pious: "He was a lover of sacrifices; he never missed the new-moon ceremonies, and he used to celebrate every festival in the cycle. One day, he wanted to take Plotinus along with him, but Plotinus said to him: 'It is up to the gods to come to me, not up to me to go to them.' We could not understand what he meant by such haughty words, and we did not dare ask him about it" (V. P. 10, 33–38). The little group of disciples seems to have been flabbergasted by this contemptuous remark about traditional religious ceremonies. But how can we fail to recognize in it Plotinus' sense of the divine presence? To find God, it is not necessary to go to the temples he is supposed to inhabit. We do not have to budge to attain his presence. Rather, we must ourselves become a living temple, in which the divine presence can manifest itself.

Moreover, God is present not only within us, but also in the world. Plotinus' last words contain yet another allusion to the two forms of divine presence. To his disciple Eustochius, who was with him in his last moments, he said, "I am trying to make what is most divine in me rise back up to what is divine in the universe." Which is as much as to say: "I am trying to die, to liberate my soul. The Life which is in me will go back to join universal Life. No longer will the screen of the body and of individuality be between them."

God, then, is total presence: the presence just as much of our self to itself as of individual beings to one another:

Since we look towards the outside, away from the point at which we are all joined together, we are unaware of the fact that we are one. We are like faces turned towards the outside, but attached on the inside to one single head. If we could turn around—either spontaneously or if we were lucky enough to "have Athena pull us by the hair"[16]—then, all at once, we would see God, ourselves, and the All. (VI 5, 7, 9–13)

16. [In Homer's *Iliad* (I, 194ff.), Achilles is about to strike his rival and commander-in-chief Agamemnon when he is restrained by the goddess Athena pulling his hair from behind. Plotinus uses the phrase to denote an unexpected divine intervention. In the preceding allusion to creatures having many faces but attached to a single head, Harder/Theiler/Beutler see a reference to Greek statues, often of Hermes, having several faces.—Trans.]

With this experience of total presence, we touch upon the most profound point of the Plotinian experience of Life. Life is total presence, since it is a simple, infinite force which diffuses itself in dynamic continuity. Plotinus seizes Life from within, as pure movement which is everywhere and unceasing. It is "already there," prior to all the particular forms it engenders, and it does not cease in them:

> The First Nature is present to all things. Present? But how? Like one single Life which is within all things. In a living being, Life does not penetrate as far as a certain point and then stop, as if it could not spread to the entire being; rather, it is present in every part of it. . . . If you can grasp the inexhaustible infinity of Life—its tireless, unwearied, unfailing nature, as if boiling over with life—it will do you no good to fix your gaze on one spot, or concentrate your attention on any given object: you will not find it there. Rather, the exact opposite would happen to you. (VI 5, 11, 37–12, 3; 12, 5, 7–11)

This is so because the movement of Life, in its total presence, cannot be fixed in any particular point. However far we go in the direction of the infinitely small or the infinitely large, the movement of life will always be beyond us, because we are *within* it. The more we seek it, the less we find. If, however, we give up seeking it, then it is there, because it is pure presence. Everything distinct which we had previously conceived or perceived only led us farther away from it:

> If you have made yourself capable of keeping pace with it; better yet, if you have come to be within the All, then you will no longer search for anything. Otherwise you will give up, be diverted to something else, and fall; although it was right there, you will not have seen it, because you were looking elsewhere. If, on the other hand, you "no longer search for anything," how will you sense its presence? Because you have approached the All, and have not just stayed within one part of it, you have not said, "I am of such-and-such dimensions," but you have dropped the "such-and-such" and have become the All. To be sure, you were already previously the All, but since something other came to be added on to you besides the "All," you were lessened by this addition. For this addition did not come from the All—what could you add to the All?—but from Not-Being. When one comes to be out of Not-Being, he is not the All, not until he rids himself of this Not-Being. Thus, you increase yourself when you get rid of everything else, and once you have gotten rid of it, the All is present to you. But if it does

come to be present . . . it will not appear to you as long as you are in the midst of other things.[17] It is not the case that it came, in order to be present; rather, if it is not present, it is you who have absented yourself. If you are absent, it is not that you have absented yourself from the All—it continues to be present—but rather that, while still continuing to be present, you have turned towards other things. (VI 5, 12, 13–29)

Life is a presence which always precedes us. As pre-existence, it is always "already there." Surely this could not be better expressed than it is in the famous *pensée* of Pascal: "You would not seek me if you had not already found me."[18]

17. Cf. Saint John of the Cross, *Ascent of Mount Carmel:* "When you pause at some particular thing, you stop abandoning yourself to the All."

18. Blaise Pascal, *Pensées,* no. 553 Brunschvicg. Reminiscences of this passage from Plotinus are frequent in Saint Augustine; for example, *Confessions* X 27, 38: "You were with me, and I was not with you." This theme recurs often in Augustine, and one may well wonder whether, in the last analysis, Pascal's famous *pensée,* which gives voice to an Augustinian doctrine, is not a distant echo of Plotinian phrases.

IV

Love

Let those who are unfamiliar with this state imagine, on the basis of their loves here down below, what it must be like to encounter the being they love most of all.

(VI 9, 9, 39ff.)

As we have seen, Plotinus' thought allows for two levels within divine reality. He shows by philosophical reasoning that, although the world of Forms is identical to that Thought which eternally thinks itself, this thought could not, as Aristotle had believed, be the principle of all things. By the mere fact that it thinks itself, thought is subject to the division between subject and object; thus a duality already lurks within its unity. Since, moreover, it is the world of Forms, this Thought contains a multiplicity and a variety which prevent it from being the primal unity. It is therefore necessary to suppose, above and beyond it, an absolute Unity: a principle so "One" that it does not even think itself.

But this is only ratiocination, and ratiocination, always remaining on the plane of consciousness and reflection, does not really allow us to know the levels of divine reality which it distinguishes. It is only a preliminary exercise, a support and a springboard. Knowledge, for Plotinus, is always experience, or rather it is an inner metamorphosis. What matters is not that we *know* rationally that there are two levels of divine reality, but that we internally raise ourselves up to these levels, and feel them within us as two different tones of spiritual life.

The world of Forms within divine Thought was, as we have seen, perceived mystically as a pure fact which can only be contemplated. In turn, we saw that this contemplation was an inner experience, a level of the self at which we come to coincide with that self-contemplation which is characteristic of divine Thought.

Now, however, Plotinus returns to the level of reflection. As he brings to mind the loving contemplation in which, fascinated by the presence of divine Life and Thought, he somehow lost himself, Plotinus now discovers, in the midst of the experience just described, the traces of an experience more profound, more intense, and more moving, albeit not yet conscious: that of love. And as he recognizes its trace, he has a premonition of something of which Intellect—that is to say, divine Life and Thought—is only the manifestation.

The spectacle of divine Life, moving in the world of Forms, inflames us with love. But why is it that we are smitten with love? What exactly is love? Can any object, however beautiful, suffice to explain the love it inspires in us? "The soul could be attracted by things which are distant from her, and far inferior to her. But when she feels an intense love for them, it is not because they are what they are, but because they have taken on something from above, in addition to what they are by themselves" (VI 7, 21, 10–13).

The reason we feel love is that some indefinable element has been added to beauty: whether movement, life, or some kind of aura, it kindles our desire, and without it beauty remains cold and inert: "Even in this world, we must say that beauty consists less in symmetry than in the light that shines upon the symmetry, and this light is what is desirable. After all, why is it that the splendor of beauty shines more brightly upon a living face while only a trace of beauty appears on the face of a dead man? . . . Why is an ugly man, as long as he is alive, more beautiful than the beauty of a statue?" (VI 7, 22, 24–32).

The world of Forms could not, by itself, kindle our love, if it did not receive from elsewhere the Life which animates it. Otherwise, the soul would remain insensitive to the beautiful proportions it contemplated: "To be sure, if the soul remains within the Intellect, it sees beautiful and venerable things, but it still does not have all that it is looking for. It is as though the soul were approaching a face which, although beautiful, was not yet capable of stimulating our sight, since there did not shine forth from it that grace which shimmers on the surface of beauty" (VI 7, 22, 22–24). The key word has been spoken: this *je ne sais quoi,* this life and movement which, when added to beauty, bring about love, are none other than grace.

Plotinus had experienced Life to be contemplation, concrete simplicity, and presence. Now, he grasps its ultimate foundation: life is
grace.

No one has understood all the implications of this Plotinian experience better than Ravaisson[1] in his *Philosophical Testament*.
Grace, he tells us there, is "eurythmia"; that is, "movement which
does well" (*"un mouvement qui fait bien"*). It can be recognized in
movements which express lack of constraint (*"l'abandon"*), defer-
ence or affability (*"la condescendance"*), or relaxation (*"la détente"*).
Artists try to grasp it in attitudes of the head, or in the feminine
smile; but one can just as easily have a premonition of it in such fundamental movements of living nature as the beating of wings or the
waves of the sea. "Observe," said Leonardo da Vinci, "the meander-
ings of each thing. If, in other words, you want to know a thing well
and depict it well, observe the type of grace that is peculiar to it."[2]

For Plotinus, if things were nothing other than what they are, in
their nature, essence and structure, they would not be lovable. In
other words, love is always superior to its object, however lofty the
latter may be. Its object can never explain or justify it. There is in
love a "something more," something unjustified; and that which, in
objects, corresponds to this "something more" is grace, or Life in its
deepest mystery. Forms and structures can be justified, but life and
grace cannot. They are "something more," and this gratuitous surplus is everything. In it, Plotinus recognizes "the trace of the Good":
"Each form, taken by itself, is [only] what it is; but it becomes desirable once the Good diffuses the color of its light over it . . . awakening love in those who desire it" (VI 7, 22, 5–7).

What Plotinus calls the Good is thus, at the same time, that
which, by bestowing grace, gives rise to love, and that which, by
awakening love, causes grace to appear. The Good is what all things
desire; it is what is desirable in an absolute sense. We asserted that
love and grace are unjustified; likewise, the Good itself is absolutely

1. [Jean Gaspard Félix Ravaisson-Mollien (1813–1900), though little known in
Anglo-American circles, had a widespread influence in the Latin Catholic world, especially as a predecessor of Bergson. Hadot's quotations are taken from Félix
Ravaisson, *Testament philosophique et fragments,* ed. Charles Devivaise (Paris,
1933).—Trans.]

2. Quoted in Ravaisson, *Testament,* p. 83.

unjustified. It is not random or accidental, but by willing itself and being what it wants to be, it freely creates the love that beings feel for it, as well as the grace they receive from it. All these formulations are, in any case, unable to translate what the soul knows of the Good when it goes through the experience of love.

Ravaisson exactly reproduces this development of Plotinus' thought. If unconstrained movement is gracious movement, this is because it reveals the nature of the creative principle. Life is grace because God is grace. The grace of things proceeds from divine goodness: "In grace, God becomes perceptible to the heart."[3]

As Bergson correctly saw, the ambiguity is essential here:

For one who contemplates the universe with the eyes of an artist, it is grace that is discerned through beauty, and goodness that is discerned through grace. Each thing manifests, in the movement that its form registers, the infinite generosity of a principle which gives itself. It is not without reason that we designate by the same word the charm we see in movement and the act of liberality characteristic of divine goodness: for M. Ravaisson, the two meanings of the word *grace* were identical.[4]

For Plotinus, too, we might add, they were identical. The grace he speaks of reveals to us the gratuitousness of divine initiative. Let the reader be reassured: this is not an attempt to Christianize Plotinus. It is too obvious that he is unaware of or opposed to the idea of a new creation in Christ, which constitutes the content of the specifically Christian concept of grace. The gratuitousness of divine initiative is only one element of this concept, and not the most characteristic one at that. If philosophical reflection goes to its own extreme, and still more if it attempts to express the content of the mystical experience, it, too, will be led to this notion of gratuitousness. It will, moreover, become clear upon reflection that all necessity and all duty presuppose the absolute initiative of an original love and freedom.

3. Ravaisson, ibid.
4. Henri Bergson, "La vie et l'oeuvre de Ravaisson." [First published in 1904, then reprinted as the introduction to Ravaisson's *Testament et Fragments,* ed. Ch. Devivaise (Paris, 1932). The work was later included by Bergson in his *La pensée et le mouvant;* cf. H. Bergson 1959, pp. 1450–81.—Trans.]

The experience of love! It is, in the first instance, the impression of an infinite transport (*élan*):

> Once the soul receives an "outflow" coming to her from the Good, she is excited and seized with Bacchic madness, and filled with stinging desires: thus love is born. Prior to this, the soul is not attracted by the Intelligence, beautiful though the latter may be, for the beauty of Intelligence is, as it were, inert before it receives the light of the Good. . . . Once, however, a "warmth" from the Good has reached her, she is strengthened and awakened; she becomes truly "winged," and although she is seized with passion for what is close to her, nevertheless she is lifted up, as if by memory, towards another, better object. As long as there is an object higher up than the current one, she keeps rising, by a natural movement, raised up by the giver of love. She rises up beyond the Spirit, yet she cannot run beyond the Good, since there is nothing lying above it. (VI 7, 22, 8–21)

Readers of Plato will have recognized in this passage many images taken from the description, in the *Symposium* and the *Phaedrus,* of that amorous emotion which leads the soul towards Beauty itself.[5]

It is true for Plotinus as well as for Plato that the ascent of the soul has its starting point in a lived amorous experience. Yet this experience is different for the two philosophers, so much so that even if Plotinus uses Plato's very terminology to describe the soul's turmoil, he does not at all invest it with the same psychological content. The amorous relation Plato speaks about is, of course, that which could be formed in ancient Greece between a master and his disciple. Whether or not Plato himself disapproved of homosexual love, Platonic love was certainly masculine in tone. The beloved was a young boy, and the lover a mature man, whether a philosopher or not. Plato tells us that the lover's love is brought on by the reflection he perceives within the beloved of Beauty itself. The soul then remembers the world of Ideas, and henceforth strives to contemplate directly— face to face and not merely in a reflection—the pure Form of Beauty. Platonic love thus starts from a very disturbing sensual emotion, but, by a discipline at the same time moral and intellectual, it attains the vision of the pure Form of Beauty in itself. At this stage the amo-

5. [As Hadot has subsequently shown in detail (P. Hadot, 1988, p. 144), this passage is crammed full of Platonic allusions and quotations, especially from the *Phaedrus,* cf. 251b2; 251d6; 254b9; 251b2–3; 254b5.—Trans.]

rous relation between lover and beloved is not destroyed, but only sublimated. The lover still loves his beloved, but now in order to guide and raise him, in his turn, to the contemplation of Beauty, so as to engender within him beautiful virtues and ideas. Once it has become spiritual, the master's love for his disciple achieves what it would always have lacked if it had remained carnal: fecundity. Nevertheless, the relation linking the lover to the Beautiful itself is utterly different from that which bound him to his beloved. With regard to the Beautiful, the lover cannot maintain the attitude of a master who loves his young disciple. It certainly seems as though, at this level, love is either transformed or left behind. Isn't love the son of "Poverty"?[6] Isn't it the sign of a deficiency?[7] Platonic love is only a means or method, each stage of which is indispensable, but which is left behind once the goal has been reached.

Plotinian love has an entirely different psychological content. We have come a long way since fourth-century-b.c. Athens. Rome—especially Imperial Rome—was hostile to "Greek love," and it horrified Plotinus himself:

> Once, the rhetor Diophanes read an apology in favor of the character Alcibiades in Plato's *Symposium,* in which he maintained that, for the sake of virtue, a disciple should submit to the amorous desires of his master. Plotinus was uncomfortable; several times, he got up as if to leave the assembly, but he contained himself and, when the audience had dispersed, he ordered me, Porphyry, to write a response. Since Diophanes refused to give me his manuscript, I had to reconstruct his arguments from memory, and I read my reply before the same audience. Plotinus was so happy with it that he kept repeating throughout the reading: "Strike so; thus you may be a light given to men."[8] (V. P. 15, 5–17)

The relations between masters and disciples in Plotinus' school were very friendly; nowhere, however, can one discern any trace of equivocal sentiments. Besides, Plotinus did not live in an exclusively masculine environment: "There were also women who were very at-

6. [According to Plato's *Symposium* 203b, Love (*Erôs*) is the offspring of *Poros* ("means," "expedient") and of *Pênia* ("poverty").—Trans.]

7. [Against the other participants in the *Symposium,* Socrates argues that *Erôs*/Love is not itself beautiful, since it is the desire for beauty and one can only desire that which one does not have.—Trans.]

8. An adapted quotation of Homer, *Iliad* 8, 282.

tached to philosophy: Gemina, owner of the house he lived in; her daughter, who bore the same name as her mother, Gemina; Amphiclea, who later became the wife of Ariston, son of Iamblichus"[9] (V. P. 9, 1–5). The psychological climate of Plotinus' school was thus profoundly different from the atmosphere of the Platonic Academy. Having determined this, however, we are still not in a position to measure the distance separating Plotinus from Plato. What is new about the Plotinian experience is that it is, first and foremost, mystical. Plato had described, in poetic, rhetorical terms, a lover's amorous agitation for his beloved: love starts out being carnal, but then, with the ascent of the soul, it serves as the motor force for an intellectual, almost scientific process. Platonic love is thus not, properly speaking, "a mystical transport."[10]

On the contrary, when Plotinus uses the language of the *Phaedrus* it is not, as it was for Plato, in order to describe human love, but rather immediately to express a mystical experience. For Plotinus, human love is no longer the starting point or first stage in a gradual ascent, but has become a mere term of comparison. It is only a reflection of that genuine love which is infused into the soul by the Good, and it disappears with the advent of the latter:

> The soul loves the Good because, from the beginning, she has been incited by the Good to love him. And the soul which has this love at hand does not wait to be reminded by the beauties of this lower world, but since she has this love—even if she does not realize it—she is constantly searching. Since she wants to rise up to the Good, the soul disdains the beauties of this world. When she sees the beautiful things in this universe, she mistrusts them, for she sees that they are in flesh and in bodies, and that they are polluted by their present dwelling place. . . . When the soul further sees that the beauties of this world flow away, she knows full well that the light which was shimmering upon them comes from elsewhere. Then the soul rises up to the other world, for she is clever at finding what she loves, and she does

9. Cf. M.-O. Goulet-Cazé, "L'arrière-plan scolaire de la *Vie de Plotin*," in L. Brisson et al. 1982, pp. 239–40. According to Goulet-Cazé, this passage shows that the "egalitarian conception between men and women which was later to become characteristic of the Neoplatonist schools" was already in effect in the school of Plotinus.

10. Cf. L. Robin, *Platon: Le banquet* (Paris: Les Belles Lettres, 1951), p. xciv. [Rather, as Robin continues, "it is a kind of ascending dialectic, since it consists . . . in climbing a *series* of stages, at each of which there occurs a unification of the particular kind of multiplicity characterizing each stage."—Trans.]

not give up before she has seized it, unless her love were somehow torn away from her. (VI 7, 31, 17–31)

As a gift of the Good, Plotinian love is immediately love of the Good. It is the invasion of the soul by a presence which leaves no room for anything but itself. But though the soul moves and is transported, this movement is not an ascent towards an end point where love ends. Plotinian love always has enough movement to go farther still; in its infinite quest, it would go beyond the Good itself if it were able to. Its terminus is the Good, not because this is a final point, but because it is the Absolute. Right from the start, the beloved was the Good, and in the experience of union, it will continue to be so.

Plotinus used Plato like Christian mystics used the *Song of Songs*. Like the latter, Plato's *Symposium* became the subject of allegorical interpretation, in which the vocabulary of carnal love was used to express a mystical experience. Indeed, the character of the "spouse" in the *Song* would fit the Plotinian soul much better than the Socrates of the *Symposium*. Plotinus much prefers feminine imagery for depicting the soul: he compares it to Psyche, to Aphrodite[11] (VI 9, 9, 26–29), to a maiden snatched away from her paternal home by an impetuous lover (VI 9, 9, 35; V 5, 12, 37).

It could rightly be objected that we ought not to be fooled by the language of mystics. They too have their commonplaces and traditional images: that is to say, their rhetoric. Moreover, the spiritual marriage between God and the soul had been one of these conventional themes at least since the time of Philo,[12] and Plato himself, who speaks of spiritual fertility, pregnancy, and giving birth, could have provided the impulse for developing these metaphors.

And yet authentic experience always gives language a special

11. [In books 4 to 6 of Apuleius' *Metamorphoses* (written c. 150 A.D.), the tale is told of Cupid and Psyche. Psyche, made to fall in love with the god of love, Cupid, becomes his lover and is shut up by him in a palace. After angering Cupid by breaking his prohibition on looking at him, Psyche manages to win back his love after many adventures, including a descent to Hades. Aphrodite was, of course, the Greek goddess of sex.—Trans.]

12. [Philo of Alexandria (c. 30B.C.–c. 45A.D.), the Hellenistic Jewish philosopher, professed in his copious writings a blend of Platonism, Stoicism, and Neo-Pythagoreanism which was highly influential both on pagan philosophers like Plotinus and on the early Christian Fathers of the Church.—Trans.]

tone, which there can be no mistaking. Experience always takes place within a given attitude and a given inner perspective. Platonic love, for example, has a masculine tonality: it is uneasy, possessive, eager to act, and hungry for posterity. It is also intimately linked to education, pedagogy, and the organization of the state. Conversely, Plotinian love has a feminine tonality, because it is first and foremost mystical. The soul "searches," "runs," and "jumps," just like the spouse of the *Song of Songs* in search of her Beloved, or Rilke's love-stricken women, with "infinite paths" opening up before them. And yet the soul also waits for the Presence to manifest itself "like the eye awaits the rising sun" (V 5, 8, 6). Platonic love rises, through a series of intellectual operations, up to the contemplation of Beauty; Plotinian love, by contrast, waits for ecstasy, ceasing all activity, establishing the soul's faculties in complete repose, and forgetting everything, so as to be completely ready for the divine invasion. The soul's highest state is complete passivity, and she tries to maintain herself in this state. Platonic love, once it has reached Beauty, displays its fertility in multiple thoughts and actions, producing science, education, and the organization of the state. Plotinian love, by contrast, refuses to return to day-to-day activity. It redescends to the world only when forced to do so by the needs of the human condition. The soul is like a virgin, who wants to stay in her Father's house (V 5, 12, 37); she is the lover who finds repose only with her Beloved. Everything other than this one necessary thing is indifferent to the soul. She does not even have the desire to tell others what she has seen: "Once one has been united to him, and has had, as it were, sufficient communion with him, *then*—if he can—let him go and announce to someone else what union is like in that other world. . . . Alternatively, if he feels that political activities are beneath him, let him remain up above, if he so desires; and this will be the conduct of one who has seen a great deal"[13] (VI 9, 7, 21–23; 26–27).

Plotinus, for his part, does not hesitate to speak to others about this union. Most of his writings are an invitation to the mystical ex-

13. [Harder/Theiler/Beutler *ad loc.*; compare Plato, *Phaedrus* 248d: when it comes time for the soul to be reincarnated, "the soul *that has seen the most* of being shall enter into a human offspring, which shall become a philosopher, a lover of beauty, or a musician or a lover."—Trans.]

perience. When he describes a state of passivity, he is inviting his readers to bring about this passivity in themselves.

□

To prepare herself for the coming of the Good, the soul must leave behind all inner activity, distinct representations, self-will, and individual possessions. The Good itself is, after all, without form:

> We will not be surprised to see the object which produces such ardent desire[14] completely free of all form, even intelligible. When the soul feels passionate love for him, she puts aside all shape she has, including whatever form of the intelligible may be within her, for it is impossible either to see him or to be adjusted with him while possessing and acting upon anything other than him. Rather, we must keep nothing else at hand—whether good or evil—so that the soul alone may receive him alone (VI 7, 34, 1–8; cf. VI 9, 7, 14).

Once the soul has no more possessions, and has stripped herself of all form, she is at one with the object of her love, and becomes the Good. She *is* the Good:

> When the soul has the good fortune to meet him, and he comes to her— rather, once he, already present, makes his presence known—when she turns away from all other things present, having made herself as beautiful as possible, and has achieved resemblance with him—just what these preparations and adornments are is obvious to those who are preparing themselves—then, suddenly, she sees him appear within her; there is no longer anything between them, and they are no longer two, but both are one. Indeed, as long as he is present, you could not tell the two of them apart; an imitation of this is when, in this world, lovers wish to be united to one another. The soul is no longer conscious of her body nor aware of being within it, and she no longer claims to be anything other than him: neither person nor animal; not individual or even the All—somehow the spectacle of such things would be lacking in uniformity[15]—and she has neither the time nor the inclination for them. Yet since it is he she has been searching for, and he is present, she goes to meet him, and she no longer looks at her-

14. [Cf., with Hadot (1988, p. 171), Plato, *Phaedrus* 250d.—Trans.]
15. [*Anômalos*. Since Plato's *Timaeus* (52e; 58a), this word was used to characterize irregularity and lack of order and control; it describes the kind of movements which agitated universal Matter before the intervention of the ordering Demiurge, and hence represents the origin of evil.—Trans.]

self, but at him. Who is it, then, that is doing the looking? She does not even take the time to see. (VI 7, 34, 8–21)

The seer . . . cannot then see or distinguish what he sees, nor does he have the impression of two entities [sc. the seer and the object seen]; rather, it is as if he has become someone else, and no longer himself. (VI 9, 10, 12–16)

If the self is thus able to coincide with the Good—which Plotinus calls the One, in order to express its absolute simplicity—the reason is that the ground or ultimate source of spiritual life is pure, simple, undecomposable presence. As we have seen, spiritual vision already had a premonition of such a total presence, behind the world of Forms; they had appeared as the manifestation of a force whose expansive movement did not stop at any particular form. Like a dancer taking up different poses, the Forms—and their Beauty—are only the figures in which the fecund simplicity of a pure movement expresses itself: a movement which engenders these forms at the same time as it goes beyond them, all the while remaining within itself. The experience of grace, as we saw, is like this too: "Beauty is nothing but fixated grace."[16] Every form, therefore, is derivative: "Form is only the trace of that which has no form; indeed, it is the latter which engenders form" (VI 7, 33, 30–31).

In mystical ecstasy, the soul leaves behind all forms, including her own, and becomes this formless reality, this pure presence which is the center of the soul, as it is of everything else.

□

While in this state, the soul has the impression of acceding to a superior form of life:

As for those unfamiliar with this state, let him[17] imagine after the model of the loves of this world what it must be like to encounter what one loves

16. Leonardo da Vinci, cited by Bergson, "Vie et oeuvre de Ravaisson," in H. Bergson 1959, p. 1472.

17. [The switch from plural to singular, like the switch a few lines below from "she" (= the soul) to "we," stands in the original Greek, and must be attributed to Plotinus' notorious insouciance about grammar.—Trans.]

most of all. Besides, these objects which we love are mortal, harmful images; they are changing, for they are not the true Beloved: they are not our Good, not what we are searching for. The true Beloved is in that other world, and it is possible to be united with him, if we participate in him and thus possess him truly, and not only from the outside, as would be the case if we only embraced him with our arms of flesh and blood. Whoever has seen knows what I am saying: when the soul approaches him, reaches him, and participates in him, she acquires another life, and when she is in this state, she realizes that the one she is with is the bestower of true life, and that she has no need of anything else; on the contrary, she knows she must reject everything else and rest in him alone. She must become him alone, cutting loose everything else we wear around ourselves.[18] Therefore we hurry to escape from here; we are irritated at the bonds which tie us to other things, so that we may embrace him with the whole of ourselves, and have no part of us which is not in contact with God. (VI 9, 9, 40–56)

In mystical union, the soul experiences a feeling of certainty, well-being, and pleasure:

At that moment, she can judge well and know that it was *him* she had been desiring; and affirm that there is nothing greater than him. In the other world, there is no possibility of deceit: where could she find something more true than the True? What she says—"It's him!"—she enunciates this later; for the moment she says it in silence. She is filled with joy, and she is not mistaken, just because she is filled with joy; she does not speak in this way because her body is tickled with pleasure,[19] but because she has become once again what she was before, when she was happy. She says she despises . . . everything which used to give her pleasure. . . . If everything else round her were to be destroyed, that would be just what she wanted, so that she could be close to him in solitude. Such is the joy to which she has acceded. (VI 7, 34, 25–39)

It is as if the Good, in its pure presence, were itself ineffable delight; and as if the soul, too, by becoming the Good, wholly became the satisfaction the Good derives from itself. In the final analysis, the Good itself is Love: "It is, at the same time, the beloved, love, and love of itself, for it is beautiful only in and for itself. . . . In

18. [I.e. the body.—Trans.]
19. [Cf., with P. Hadot (1988; p. 172), Plato, *Phaedrus* 251c.—Trans.]

it, being and its desire for itself are one. . . . It is itself that which it loves; which is to say, it brings itself into existence" (VI 8, 15, 1–8; 16, 14).

□

Divine reality thus appears to us under two aspects, according to the level of our inner life. Sometimes, we contemplate nothing but the Good, that universe of Forms which think themselves and live within the Intellect. At other times, the Beautiful, which embellishes the Intellect with its grace, overwhelms us with its love. The Good is therefore superior to the Beautiful: "The Good is gentle, mild, and very delicate, and always at the disposition of whomever desires it. The Beautiful, by contrast, provokes awestruck terror and astonishment, and the pleasure it causes is mixed with pain. Indeed, the Beautiful leads those who do not know it far away from the Good, like a lover entices his fiancée away from the house of her father" (V 5, 12, 33–37).

If the Beautiful were all there was, we would be seduced, fascinated, and, ultimately, terrified. Until the soul has had a premonition of the presence of the Good behind the Beautiful, and until grace has come along to make the fascinating immobility of the Beautiful gentle enough for her eyes to bear, the soul is terrified[20] when she contemplates the world of Forms.

Did Plotinus sense the disconcerting, enigmatic aspect of the spectacle of universal Life? Did he feel what Rilke expressed in his first *Elegy,* that "Beauty is only the first stage of the terrible"?

Perhaps: but for Plotinus, overwhelming majesty is only the first stage of divine reality. If God appears to us in this way, it is because we have not yet raised ourselves up high enough. For one who has had the experience of divine love, the source of all things appears as "gentle, mild, and very delicate," and it is only natural that all things

---

20. [*Thambos echei* (V 5, 12, 35). *Thambos* designates a kind of "sacred terror which one feels at the approach of a person or object charged with supernatural force"; cf. in the New Testament Mark 1:27; Mark 10:32; Luke 4:36; Luke 5:9, etc. (A.-J. Festugière, "La religion grecque," in *Histoire générale des religions,* Paris: Quillet, 1960, vol. 1, p. 477.—Trans.]

should reflect its grace and its beauty.[21] Plotinus' spiritual life consists in tranquil confidence and peaceful gentleness. The terrors of the Gnostics seem ridiculous to him: "Let them abandon the tragic tone they adopt when they talk about the so-called dangers of the celestial spheres, which in reality 'provide all joys for mortal men'"[22] (II 9, 13, 6–8).

□

In the last analysis, divine gentleness is light, and for Plotinus, this helps us to understand many things. First of all, it is in the form of light that pure presence invades us:

Suddenly, a light bursts forth, pure and alone. We wonder whence it came: from the outside, or from the inside? Once it disappears, we say, "It was inside—and yet, no, it wasn't inside." We must not try to learn whence it comes, for here there is no "whence." The light comes from nowhere, and it goes nowhere; it simply either appears or does not appear. That is why we must not chase after it, but quietly wait for it to appear, preparing ourselves to be spectators, as the eye waits for the rising sun. Then the sun appears over the horizon—"coming out of Ocean," as the poets say—and allows the eye to behold it. . . . He, however, did not come, as one might have expected, but he came as though without having come, for he was seen, not as something having come, but as something already present before everything else, even before the coming of Spirit. . . . What a wonder! He is present, and yet he did not come! He is nowhere; and yet there is no place in which he is not present! One may, indeed, be astonished in this way at first; but whoever knows him would rather be astonished by the contrary; rather, it is impossible that the contrary should happen, so that there is no occasion to be astonished. (V 5, 7, 33–8, 5; 8, 13–16; 23–27)

21. We find the same two stages once more in Saint John of the Cross, "Spiritual Canticle," in *Collected Works,* p. 460: "[These raptures and terrors] are experienced in such visits by those who have not yet reached the stage of perfection, but are advancing along in the state of proficients. Those who have reached perfection receive all communications in peace and gentle love. These raptures then cease, for they are communications preparatory to the reception of the total communication."

22. [An adapted quote from Pindar's *First Olympian Ode,* line 30, in which it is "Grace" (*Charis*) that does the providing. Some Gnostic sects held that after death the soul would have to ascend through the celestial spheres, each of which was guarded by a demon or series of demons. The only way of getting past them was to know the

For Plotinus, as for Plato,[23] vision consists in contact between the
inner light of the eye and exterior light. Yet Plotinus concludes from
this that when vision becomes spiritual, there is no longer any distinction between inner and outer light. Vision is light, and light is
vision. There is a kind of self-vision of light, in which light is, as it
were, transparent to itself.

In this world, certain visual phenomena allow us to imagine such
a unity of vision and light:

> It is not always a foreign, exterior light which the eye knows; sometimes,
> before the exterior light, it beholds in an instant, a light more brilliant and
> akin to itself. Sometimes it leaps forth from it in the darkness at night; at
> others the eye does not wish to look at any other thing, it shuts its eyelids
> before it, and yet still emits light. Finally, if one presses down on his eye, he
> sees the light within it. In this case, he sees without seeing; and it is then that
> he sees more than ever, for what he is seeing is light. Other things are only
> luminous, but they are not light itself. (V 5, 7, 23–31)

In the mystical experience, the inner eye of the soul sees nothing
but light:

> Carried off, as it were, by the wave of the Spirit itself, lifted up high by it,
> as if it were swollen, "he suddenly saw, without seeing how."[24] But the spec-
> tacle, filling the eyes with light, did not cause some other object to be seen
> by its means; rather, what was seen was light itself. It is not that there were
> two things within it: on the one hand a visible object, and on the other its
> light, nor was there the Spirit and then what is thought by the Spirit; there is
> only a dazzling light, which engenders all these things later on. (VI 7, 36,
> 17–23)

The soul's vision becomes indistinguishable from this original
brilliance. It is as if the soul were seeing the light at the very center of
its own vision:

---

appropriate password, the memorization of which was a vital part of Gnostic
teaching.—Trans.]

23. [On Plato's theory of vision cf. *Republic* 507cff.: clearly Plotinus' main source
of inspiration in both the preceding and the following passage.—Trans.]

24. [As the author has since pointed out (P. Hadot 1988; p. 177 n. 322), this is a
probable reminiscence of Homer, *Odyssey* 5, 390–93, in which Odysseus, adrift for
three days after a dangerous storm, finally glimpses the land of the Phaiakians "lying
very close to him/as he took a sharp look, *lifted high on the top a great wave.*" The
passage is dense with other literary allusions, especially to Plato's *Republic* (505a2)
and *Symposium* (210e3–4).—Trans.]

We must believe that we have seen him when, suddenly, the soul is filled
with light; for this light comes from him and is identical with him. We must
also consider that he is present when, like another god someone might sum-
mon into his house, he comes, and illuminates it. He would not have caused
this illumination if he had not come. Similarly, the soul when she is unillu-
minated is godless and bereft of him; once she has been illuminated, however, she has what she was looking for. *This* is the real goal for the soul: to
touch and to behold this light itself, by means of itself. She does not wish to
see it by means of some other light; what she wants to see is that light by
means of which she is able to see. What she must behold is precisely that by
which she was illuminated. . . . How, then, could this come about? Eliminate everything [sc. that is not light]! (V 3, 17, 28–38)

What we must see is that which allows us to see: light, to be sure,
but just as much the original act of vision: in other words, that which
sees in the depth of our vision.[25] If life, in all its stages, is vision, it is
because pure presence, which is its center and its source, is, in a
sense, absolute vision, the immediate transparency of the Good to
itself: "In a sense, for it, its being is its act of looking at itself" (VI 8,
16, 20–21).

The Plotinian experience constantly expresses itself in terms of
light, brightness, transparency, brilliance, and illumination. Can we
conclude from this that Plotinus was unaware of the darkness and
nights of the spirit which characterize Christian mysticism? On the
contrary: insofar as inner emptiness and abnegation—"Eliminate
everything that is not light"—may appear to the soul as a kind of
night, in that she has the impression of losing the light she is used to,
we must admit that there is also a mystical night for Plotinus. However, insofar as the night of the Christian mystics corresponds to the
exercise of faith, even to the point of becoming one with the suffering of the crucified Christ, abandoned by the Father, it is obvious
that all this is absent from Plotinus. For him, one single Life, simple
and luminous, flows through all things. It is enough to set aside the
Forms, which conceal it as they express it, in order for this Life to
make us feel its presence.

25. How Plotinian was Goethe's reply to Schopenhauer when the latter ex-
pounded to him an Idealist theory of vision: "What! Light is only present when you
see it? No! It is rather *you* who would not be here if light itself did not see you."
(*Goethes Gespräche*, ed. Biedermann [Leipzig: 1909], vol. 2, p. 245).

V

Virtues

Without true virtue, God is only a word.
(II 9, 15, 39)

Why, then, do we not remain up there?
(VI 9, 10, 1)

This is *the* great Plotinian question. There is a part of ourselves which is always up above, and if, sometimes, we are fortunate enough to be raised up to this higher level, it is then that we live the best of lives. We then rest within the Divine; we are overcome by total presence, experience the love of the Good, and become an act of vision which is nothing other than the very light from which vision emanates. If this is the case, how is it that we come back down? How can presence become absence? How can the flame of love be snuffed out (cf. VI 9, 9, 60)? How can we perceive distinct objects once again, regain consciousness, reflect, think rationally, perceive our bodies? How is it, in other words, that we become human beings again?

Once one has experienced that genuine life is up above, and tasted, in a fleeting flash, of divine union, how can one return to day-to-day life? This life may seem normal to other people, but now, for one who has known ecstasy, it appears as a violent and abnormal state.

If we fall back down, it must be because we could not stand being up above any longer. From now on, however, we won't be able to stand being down here. Henceforth, we don't belong anywhere: we are too terrestrial to be able to keep the divine gift, but have now become too divine to forget it: "Souls necessarily become, as it were, amphibious,[1] alternately living the life up above and the life here down below" (IV 8, 4, 31–33).

---

1. [There is an etymological pun here: the Greek words *amphi,* meaning "of both kinds," and *bios,* "life," being combined to form *amphibioi,* "living a double life." As in

64

Such is the paradox of the human condition. When we are up above, we *are* ourselves, but we no longer *belong to* ourselves, because this state has been bestowed upon us and we are not in control of it. In this world, we *think* we belong to ourselves, but we know that we no longer really *are* ourselves.

The discontinuity between these levels cannot be abolished. Once we have been up above, we do, after all, have to resume our normal lives: we must look after our bodies and other people, think rationally, make provisions for the future. Yet although the mystical experience was transitory, this does not mean that we can forget it. Once we've experienced it, we are never quite the same again.

How, then, should we live? For Plotinus, the great problem is to learn how to live our day-to-day life. We must learn to live, after contemplation, in such a way that we are once again prepared for contemplation. We must concentrate ourselves within, gathering ourselves together[2] to the point that we can always be ready to receive the divine presence, when it manifests itself again. We must detach ourselves from life down here to such an extent that contemplation can become a continuous state. Nevertheless, we still have to learn how to put up with day-to-day life; better still, we must learn to illuminate it with the clear light that comes from contemplation. For this, in turn, a lot of work is required: interior purification, simplification, and unification.

This is the task of virtue, of the importance of which Plotinus, as he grew older, became more and more aware. While the treatises of his youth and maturity, though they do recommend the practice of virtue, are primarily hymns to the beauty of the spiritual world and the intoxication of ecstasy, the works he wrote near the end of his life are devoted almost exclusively to ethical subjects.

The experience of divine union remains at the center of his

English, so in Greek the term was normally used to designate animals, especially frogs.—Trans.]

2. ["Se recueillir," a technical term of spirituality. Robert's dictionary s.v. "recueillement" defines it as "the action or fact of concentrating one's thought on spiritual life, in complete detachment from mundane preoccupations." Literally, the word means "to gather; collect from various sources"; one thinks of the English expression "to gather/collect one's thoughts." This meaning was already active, in a quite literal sense, for the Neoplatonists. For Plotinus' disciple Porphyry, the way to prepare one-

thought. But from now on Plotinus concentrates on showing how virtue, born from this union, transforms one's entire being and becomes substantial wisdom. Any contemplation which had no effect on concrete life, and did not culminate in rendering man similar to God through virtue, would remain foreign and meaningless to us.

This, as Plotinus was well aware, is the danger of Gnosticism. Those who know themselves to be saved by nature tend to believe moral effort will make no substantial difference. Besides, the Gnostic is not of this world, not really "from here." What good is it, then, to practice virtues, since all one has to do to insure salvation is to wait for the end of the world? It is useless and impossible to try to live, down here below, according to our spiritual nature. Here Plotinus recognizes one of the gravest dangers of the spiritual life:

> They never make mention of virtue, but omit the subject completely. They neither say what virtue is, nor how many kinds of virtue there are, nor do they make mention of the many fine treatments of the subject to be found in the works of the ancients. . . . Neither do they say how the soul can be purified and cured. For it does no good to say, "Look towards God," unless we are taught *how* to look towards him. . . . What is there to stop us, someone might say, from looking towards God without abstaining from any pleasure, and without suppressing our anger? What is to stop us, let us say, from keeping the name "God" in mind, and yet being kept ensnared by every passion, and not trying to eliminate any of them? What shows God to us is virtue, as it comes to be in the soul, accompanied by wisdom. Without this genuine virtue, God is only a word. (II 9, 15, 28–40)

Gnosis, or pure knowledge, cannot lead us to God if it is only a doctrine, a theory, or a theology. This is so even if it employs the traditional methods of "negative theology": "What instructs us about him are analogies, negations, knowledge about the beings which derive from Him, and certain *rungs*."[3] Yet the only thing that

---

self for the ascent to one's true self was "by gathering together all your spiritual limbs, currently dispersed and fragmented" (*Letter to Marcella* 10, p. 111, 11–12 Des Places.—Trans.]

3. [*Anabasmoi*. Cf., with P. Hadot 1988 (176 n. 317), Plato, *Symposium* 211c: "This is the way, the only way, the candidate must approach . . . the sanctuary of Love. Starting from individual beauties, the quest for the universal beauty must find him ever mounting the heavenly ladder, stepping from rung to rung (*epanabasmois*)"—Trans.]

will lead us to God is the inner transformation of our being, obtained through virtue: "But what lead us to him are purifications, virtues, and inner adornments; stepping stones[4] towards the Intelligible; taking up our abode there; and the feasts we celebrate up above" (VI 7, 36, 6–10).

The mystical experience is far from being just idle chatter or a dream. Plotinus vigorously combats the illusion of Gnostic quietism. It is not enough to tell people: "You are of a divine race." Mere assertions cannot transform the inner soul unless they are accompanied by the genuine practice of virtue. Those who despise virtue also despise the demands proper to human nature. And "He who would act the angel acts the beast":[5]

We must not exalt ourselves in a boorish way, but with moderation, and without raising ourselves higher up than our nature is able to make us rise; we must not rank ourselves alone after God, but recognize that there is room for other beings in his presence besides ourselves; otherwise, we are merely *flying in a dream*[6] and depriving ourselves of the possibility of becoming like God, as far as this is possible for a human soul. And it *is* possible for her, if she is guided by the Intellect. *To go beyond the Intellect is in fact to fall beneath it.* Men of little sense are persuaded when, all of a sudden, they hear words like these: "You will be better than everyone: not only human beings but gods as well!" for arrogance is widespread among mankind. If a person who had previously been humble, mediocre, and ordinary were to hear: "You are the son of God; those others, whom you used to hold in awe, are not sons of God" . . . then do you really think other people are going to join in the chorus? (II 9, 9, 45–60)

□

Plotinian virtue is born of contemplation, and brings us back to contemplation:

When one falls from contemplation, he must reawaken the virtue within him. When he perceives himself as embellished and brought into order by

4. [*Epibaseis.* Cf. Plato, *Republic* 511b.—Trans.]
5. ["Qui veut faire l'ange fait la bête": a quotation from Pascal's *pensée* no. 358, the full text of which reads: "Man is neither angel nor beast; and the misfortune is that he who would act the angel acts the beast."—Trans.]
6. [Cf., with H/T/B, Plato, *Theaetetus* 158b: "I cannot undertake to deny that madmen and dreamers believe what is false, when madmen imagine they are gods or dreamers think they have wings and are flying in their sleep."—Trans.]

these virtues, he will be made light again,[7] and will proceed, through virtue, to Intellect and wisdom; then, through wisdom, to the One. Such is the life of the gods and of divine and happy men:[8] release from the things down here below, a life which takes no pleasure in earthly things, a solitary flight to the Solitary One. (VI 9, 11, 46–51)

Such is the soul's itinerary. Lifted up as far as the One by the latter's liberal, gracious motion, the soul is not able to maintain herself at the summit of herself, and falls back down again. Once back in practical life, consciousness, and discursive thought, however, she rediscovers within herself, here down below, virtue: that trace of God which makes her similar to God. By the practice of the virtues, the soul can rise up once more to the Intellect; in other words, to a purely spiritual life. Once she reaches this state of perfection, virtue becomes wisdom: a stable state form which the soul may once again render herself ready for divine union.

Virtue comes back into play once the soul, no longer able to maintain herself at the level of the Spirit, falls from contemplation. It might be objected that the soul had already been purified, before she was able to contemplate. Here, however, we once again come across the paradox of divine presence: "You would not seek me if you had not already found me."[9] Virtue, which leads us to God, can only be born in the soul as the result of an initial union with God: "Life in the other world is the activity of the Intellect, and this activity, in peaceful contact with him, engenders beauty, justice, and virtue; for once the soul has been filled by God, she is pregnant with these things" (VI 9, 9, 17–20).

Virtue cannot be born in the soul until she has glimpsed—even if only for an instant—the Beauty of the Intellect, and has tasted, even

---

7. [*Kouphisthêsetai*. In the eschatology of Plato's *Phaedrus* (248cff.), disincarnate souls follow the chariots of the gods in the supracelestial realm. Should they be guilty of forgetfulness or wrongdoing, they are said to "lose their wings" and "become heavy," and fall down to earth and incarnation in a terrestrial body. Those souls who live righteously—preferably as philosophers—can, after three earthly lifetimes, "regain their plumage" and "be borne aloft" (*kouphizesthai*) to a celestial place of beatitude.—Trans.]

8. [Cf. Plato, *Theaetetus* 176a: "Discourse . . . that will rightly celebrate the life of gods and of happy men" (H/T/B).—Trans.]

9. [Cf. above, p. 47.—Trans.]

if only in the flash of an instant, the joy of divine union. To be sure, since she is not sufficiently purified, the soul cannot sustain these states; but it is precisely the main task of virtue to purify the soul so that she can endure divine union continuously.

Nevertheless, the initial movement towards virtue is already the divine gift of illumination and the experience of unity. How could the soul know that there is a part of her that remains up above if she had not become conscious of it? How could she desire to make herself similar to God if she had not, all of a sudden, experienced divine presence?

The soul receives into herself an outpouring that comes from above. (VI 7, 22, 8)

The soul loves the Good because, since the beginning, it has incited her to love it. (VI 7, 31, 17)

The illumination which comes from the Intellect gives the soul a clearer, brighter life, but a life which is not generative. On the contrary, it turns the soul back upon herself and does not allow her to become dispersed, but rather makes her satisfied with the splendor within her. (V 3, 8, 27–31)

Moreover, Plotinian virtue maintains the character of its origin. It wants to be a true assimilation to God.

This is why Plotinus distinguishes two degrees in the virtues. There are the virtues one could call "social": prudence, justice, strength, and temperance. At this level, these social virtues merely moderate the passions which come from the body, and they regulate our relations with other human beings. Above these social virtues are the purificatory virtues. Through these, the soul, instead of forming a composite whole with the body—which is what the social virtues promote—separates herself radically from it and turns all her attention towards God. These two movements are, moreover, inseparable (I 2, 4, 16).

The two degrees of virtues correspond to two different levels of human reality. There is the "composite"; that is, that part of ourselves which corresponds to a kind of mixture of the soul and the body. It is here that passions, fears, desires, pain, and pleasure are produced. Above this level there is the pure soul: the inner or spiritual man, whose proper activity is thinking, or more precisely contemplating God. The lower virtues regulate the activity of the "composite," but the sage refuses to identify himself with this "composite." This living body, with its passions, pains, and pleasures, may *belong to* him, but they are not *identical with* him.

> The true person is something different, pure from contact with the animal part of our nature. He possesses the virtues which consist in thought, and which establish themselves in the soul which is separating itself from the body—or rather, which, while separating itself, is already separate while still remaining in this world. (I 1, 10, 7–10)

Thus the purificatory virtues correspond to a complete transformation of inner life, in which one could say that all our spiritual energy flows back inside and upwards. The sage lives at the summit of himself, only giving to his lower levels the attention necessary for the conservation of life. At this stage, moral effort is no longer a combat, but a victorious flight. Lower things are no longer of interest; we don't really pay attention to them anymore, and they therefore no longer present a problem. All our activity is turned towards God.

It need scarcely be pointed out that Plotinus goes to this highest level right from the start. From his point of view, the social virtues no longer have a raison d'être, since the moral problems they were supposed to solve have been eliminated: "He who possesses the higher virtues . . . arrives at higher principles and measures, and will act in accordance with these. For example, he does not postulate temperance as moderation; rather, he detaches himself completely, insofar as this is possible. He does not live the life of a man, even of a good man, as the latter is defined by civic virtue. He leaves this kind of life behind, and chooses another: the life of the gods" (I 2, 7, 22–28).

"The life of the gods": an appropriate term, since the purificatory virtues, as they turn the soul towards God alone, imitate the movement by which God rests within himself: "Wisdom and prudence consist in the contemplation of that which exists within the Intellect. . . . The best kind of justice for the soul is when her activity is directed entirely towards the Intellect, while temperance is turning inwards towards the Intellect. Bravery is impassability, in imitation of that which the soul looks at: the Intellect, which is impassible by nature" (I, 2, 6, 12–13; 23–26).

Like Nature, Plotinian virtue is entitled to say, "Born of contemplation, I love contemplation, . . . and I contemplate" (III 8, 4, 6).

This is not at all surprising, since for Plotinus all life, in the last analysis, is contemplation. Once separated from the body and turned towards God, what else is the soul to do but contemplate? "What is virtue for the soul? It is what she obtains as a result of her conversion. And what is this? Contemplation" (I 2, 4, 17–19).

In every sense of the word, then, virtue is the continuation of contemplation. Born of contemplation and returning to contemplation, Plotinian virtue is nothing but contemplation. It is the effort of attention through which the soul tries to maintain herself at the level to which God has raised her. Once it has become the state known as wisdom, contemplation will become perpetual.

Plotinus had asked, "Why, then, do we not remain up above?" But he had immediately supplied the answer: "Because we have not yet completely left this place" (VI 9, 10, 1).

That is to say, because we are not yet sufficiently purified by virtue. He had gone on to say, "But there will come a time when contemplation will be continuous, and the body will no longer present any obstacle" (VI 9, 10, 2–3).

Plotinian virtue, then, consists in an extremely simple spiritual attitude. When we consider it from the outside, we can no doubt distinguish different aspects in it, which we may then call prudence, justice, strength, or temperance. Seen from within, however, it is not even an effort to separate oneself from the body; it is only a continuous attention to the divine, and a perpetual exercise of God's presence. We could, if we wished, speak of a metamorphosis of our way of seeing. Plotinian virtue wants to see nothing other than the divine presence, in itself, around itself, and throughout all things.

By dint of the exercise of God's presence, divine union becomes continuous. Contemplation of the world of Forms and the experience of the love of the Good are no longer rare and extraordinary events. They give way to a state of union which is in a sense substantial, as it seizes our being in its entirety:

As for the activities of the sage relating to contemplation: some, indeed, might perhaps be hindered [sc. by outside circumstances]; namely, those [pronouncements] which he would utter only after inquiry and examination. Yet the "greatest lesson"[10] is always near at hand and present for him; all the more so if he were inside the so-called "bull of Phalaris."[11] It is vain to call such a situation pleasant, whether they repeat it twice or many times, for according to them, the person claiming "this is pleasant" is the same as the one in a situation of agony. For us, however, the person who suffers is one thing, the person speaking is another. Although this other is forced to live with the sufferer, yet he will never leave off the contemplation of the Good in its entirety. (I 4, 13, 3–12)

Inside the bull of Phalaris, the Plotinian sage will not deny that he is suffering. But the appalling suffering of the body, even when perceived by the soul, never reaches higher than the lower levels of the self. Turned towards God and concentrated at the summit of herself, the Plotinian soul continues to contemplate, and cannot divert her attention away to the inferior part of herself which is plunged in suffering. God, to whom she is united, is the Good. What more can she desire? What can adversity, the deprivation of pleasures, or even suffering, matter to her? She has everything; she *is* everything, and nothing else matters. God alone is enough.

Such is the wisdom of Plotinus. It is a mystical wisdom, which has no meaning for whomever has not experienced divine union.

So far, we have looked at Plotinian thought from the inside, as it

10. [*To megiston mathêma.* Cf. Plato, *Republic* 505a: "You have often heard that the greatest thing to learn (*megiston mathêma*) is the Idea of the Good by reference to which just things and all the rest become useful and beneficial." For the Neoplatonists the terms Good and One are used interchangeably to designate the first principle. For the sage to have knowledge of the Idea of Good "near at hand" (*procheiron*) means that he can, thanks to assiduous exercise, call it to mind at each and every moment, realize the identity of the best part of himself with the Principle of all things, and thereby become indifferent to external circumstances.—Trans.]

11. [Phalaris, tyrant of Agrigentum in Sicily, used to have his victims burned alive inside a bronze bull. According to the Stoics and Epicureans, the wise man would still be happy even inside the bull of Phalaris (Cf. Cicero, *Tusculan Disputations* 2, 17; Usener *Epicurea* 601.—Trans.] In the next lines, Plotinus is alluding to the Epicureans ("It is vain to call such a situation pleasant"). The Epicureans made no distinction between the purely spiritual self and the corporeal self; they conceded the existence only of the corporeal self. If the corporeal self is completely overwhelmed by suffering, it cannot, says Plotinus, at the same time affirm that it is in a pleasant state. We must assume that it is the spiritual self, constantly submerged in the contemplation of the Good, which makes this assertion.

were. There is no doubt that, as he leads us to discover the levels of the self, the beauty of universal life, the love of the Good, and purifying virtue, Plotinus is revealing to us his innermost experience. The time now seems to have come to consider Plotinus' attitudes from the *outside*. We must ask his biographer Porphyry to tell us in what way Plotinus concretely resolved the problem he set forth at the beginning of this chapter: how can we live down here in this world once we have contemplated divine Beauty and felt the love of the Good? Better yet, how can we live, while still down here below, in continuous contemplation?

Gentleness

> The Good is gentle, mild, and very delicate, and always at the disposition
> of whomever desires it.
>
> (V 5, 12, 33–34)

The modern reader who opens Porphyry's *Life of Plotinus*[1] cannot
help but feel a certain uneasiness. He is taken aback by its very first
sentence: "Plotinus resembled someone ashamed of being in a
body" (V. P. I, 1).

Throughout the following pages, we encounter a bizarre character who refuses to talk about his parents, his homeland (V. P. I, 3),
and his date of birth (ibid. 2, 37), and who cannot stand to have his
portrait made (I, 4).

Later on, Porphyry does not hesitate to go into realistic details:

> Although he often suffered from colic, he would not submit to an enema,
> saying that it was not suitable for a man of his age to submit to such treat-
> ment, nor would he consent to take antidotes consisting of theriac,[2] saying
> that he did not even touch food made from the bodies of domestic animals.
> He avoided the bath, and instead had himself massaged at home every day.
> When the plague increased in severity, however, it so happened that his
> masseurs died, and he neglected this treatment. (V. P. 2, 1–9)

After an account—extremely moving, moreover—of Plotinus' final sickness and death, Porphyry transmits to us a few biographical
details which the master had confided to him in the course of var-

---

1. Richard Harder's recent German translation of the *Life of Plotinus,* in *Plotins
Schriften* vol. Vc, Hamburg: Meiner, 1958, represents a considerable improvement
over the translation of Emile Bréhier. I have utilized it frequently in this chapter. [I
have also taken into account the translation of A. H. Armstrong (*Plotinus* vol. 1, pp. 3–
85; see Bibliography); as well as the information and partial translations provided by
L. Brisson et al. 1982. Unfortunately, the companion volume, containing a completely new translation of the *Life of Plotinus,* appeared too late for me to use: see now
Porphyre, La vie de Plotin: Etudes d'introduction, texte grec et traduction française, L.
Brisson, M.-O. Goulet-Cazé et al., Paris: Vrin, 1992.—Trans.]

2. Theriac contained the flesh of wild animals, in particular snakes.

ious conversations. In particular, he mentions the following odd childhood reminiscence: "Even though he was already going to school, and was eight years old, he still used to go to his nursemaid, and uncover her breasts so as to suckle. When he heard it said that he was an awful little boy, however, he was ashamed and gave up the practice"[3] (V. P. 3, 2–6).

Immediately afterwards, we switch to the episode of Plotinus' encounter with his master Ammonius, and then to "The Adventures of Plotinus in the East":

> From the day he met him, Plotinus remained with Ammonius uninterruptedly: he penetrated so deeply into philosophy that he was anxious to gain experience of the philosophy which is practiced among the Persians, and which has been perfected by the Indians. When the emperor Gordian[4] was preparing to attack the Persians, Plotinus enlisted in the army and went along with them. He was then already thirty-nine, having studied under Ammonius for eleven whole years. When Gordian was killed in Mesopotamia, Plotinus escaped with difficulty, and took refuge in Antioch. When Philip[5] acceded to power, Plotinus, at the age of forty, came to Rome. (V. P. 3, 13–24)

From this moment on, we see Plotinus gradually becoming the head of a philosophical school. Yet philosophy near the end of Antiquity was, more than anything else, a way of life. One went into philosophy, so to speak, as one went into religion: as the result of a conversion which brought about a complete change of one's existence. The philosopher was less a professor than a spiritual guide: he exhorted his charges to conversion, and then directed his new converts—often adults as well as young people—to the paths of

3. Out of all his childhood, why did Plotinus only mention to Porphyry this one single anecdote? Was this a case of psychological trauma? In itself, the phenomenon of late weaning is very frequent in the East. If Plotinus told this story, it was perhaps to give an example of an involuntary misdeed, of the kind that the sage can still commit even when he has attained perfection (cf. I 2, 6, 4).

4. [Gordian III, born 225 A.D., emperor from 238–44. Although successful in his campaign against the Persians (launched in 242), Gordian was assassinated in a coup led by his praetorian prefect Philip the Arab (see following note).—Trans.]

5. [Julius Verus Philippus, known as Philip the Arab, emperor 244–49. After the death of Gordian, Philip concluded peace with the Persians and returned to Rome. He was killed in the course of the civil war against his own praetorian prefect and eventual successor, Decius.—Trans.]

wisdom. He was a spiritual adviser.[6] To be sure, he did some teaching, and his classes could even be rather technical, dealing with questions of logic or physics. These intellectual exercises, however, were only part of a method of education directed towards the soul in its entirety.

This, then, is how Plotinus appears to us in Porphyry's narration. Porphyry describes for us Plotinus' method of teaching, lists the disciples who surrounded him, and tells us a few very lively anecdotes. Above all, he speaks to us of his master with admiration: "The attention (*prosochê*) he paid to himself never let up, except during his sleep. He did not, moreover, get much of the latter, owing to the scanty food he consumed—often he would not even touch bread—and because his thought was continually turned towards the Intellect" (V. P. 8, 20–23).

As we said, on reading all this, a modern reader—even one well versed in the knowledge of Antiquity—experiences a certain uneasiness. This impression is well epitomized by an expert who knew his Plotinus inside out, Emile Bréhier. He writes:

Certainly the moral health and equilibrium one finds in the school of Epictetus is lacking in Plotinus' milieu. In it, we can see disturbing symptoms of fatigue and nervous exhaustion. The "flight from the world," that constant theme of Plotinian preaching, bears a striking resemblance to the "running away from life," that constant need to move on, "to go anywhere, as long as it is out of the world," which, according to Dr. Pierre Janet, are the symptoms of the melancholic syndrome. The rather abrupt way in which Plotinus left Alexandria, never to return, and his complete detachment from his family and his country, can perhaps be explained by this nervous state, which was, of course, maintained by the deplorable diet to which he adhered. Not only did he abstain from meat like a Pythagorean, but he did not take the most elementary precautionary hygienic measures. Add to that intellectual overwork, which was frequent in his school; his constantly strained meditation, which shows itself in a style in which the thoughts flow without a break, and more quickly, as it were, than the words; and the lack of

6. [*Directeur de conscience.* In French Catholic religiosity, this term designates a priest chosen to advise a person in matters spiritual, moral, and religious. On the function of the pagan spiritual guide, cf. I. Hadot, "The Spiritual Guide," in A. H. Armstrong, ed., *Classical Mediterranean Spirituality, Egyptian Greek, Roman,* London: Routledge and Kegan Paul, 1986, pp. 436–59.—Trans.]

sleep which was its consequence: all this, in the long run, ruined his health. By the time Porphyry knew him, Plotinus' stomach was in a sorry state, and his eyesight very weak. He suffered from a chronic throat ailment, and a skin disease. Above all, he had a kind of complacency—in itself morbid—towards states of ill-health: "Man must diminish and weaken his body, in order to show that *the true man* is quite different from exterior things. . . . He will not wish to be completely unfamiliar with suffering; he will even *want* to experience suffering" (I 4, 14, 12–14; 21–23).

Bréhier continues: "This remarkable philosophical testament goes beyond Stoic indifference, since it goes so far as actually to desire pain."[7]

For his part, Dr. Gillet, who diagnoses the symptoms of pulmonary tuberculosis in Plotinus' final illness, recognizes the psychological symptoms of this disease in Plotinus' spiritual attitude, while in the philosophy of Plotinus he sees the ideal of a sick man.[8]

In this way, we wind up making a kind of pagan Pascal out of Plotinus: someone living in a state of perpetual tensions and suffering, and seeing in sickness the normal state of mankind.

□

Many of the features of this gloomy portrait have been exaggerated. The anecdotes narrated by Porphyry have often been wrongly interpreted, the information he gives us poorly understood, and even his silences taken as detrimental to Plotinus. If we reread his account carefully, a wholly different Plotinus may appear before us.

First of all, we must resign ourselves to not knowing a great deal about Plotinus' life. Porphyry lived with him for only six years. He did not meet him until near the end of his life, at a moment when he was getting old, and was beginning to show signs of his final illness. The picture Porphyry gives us is necessarily a partial one. Plotinus' past was an almost complete blank to him, and he was naturally led to emphasize the ascetic—and at the same time unhealthy—aspect of the Master's life.

Porphyry simply tells us too little about Plotinus' youth for us to

7. Emile Bréhier, *Plotin: Les Ennéades,* vol. 1, Paris: Les Belles Lettres, 1924, pp. vii–ix.
8. P. Gillet, *Plotin au point de vue médical et psychologique,* medical thesis, Paris, 1934.

be able to interpret it psychologically and discover in it the traces of a "melancholic syndrome." *Pace* Bréhier, nothing in Porphyry's story permits us to assert that Plotinus left Alexandria abruptly, or that he abandoned Ammonius in order to follow Gordian on his march towards Persia. We could just as easily suppose that it was Ammonius himself who advised Plotinus to make this philosophical expedition, this "pilgrimage to the source" of Oriental wisdom, which had fascinated Greek philosophers since the most ancient times. What is not clear from Porphyry's story is how Plotinus was able to get himself introduced into the circle of the emperor Gordian. As Richard Harder has remarked,[9] there are political underpinnings to Plotinus' adventure which elude our understanding. For Plotinus to have been able to participate in this expedition and accompany the emperor, he must already have had close relations with the senators who had access to the emperor. Moreover, Plotinus' flight after the assassination of Gordian confirms this hypothesis. Gordian was killing during an uprising of his soldiers, as a result of which the usurper Philip took power. Plotinus, then, fled—with the utmost difficulty—because he was involved with the supporters of the emperor Gordian. We do not know why he then went to Rome, rather than, for example, to Athens. But when he did arrive in the capital of the Empire, Plotinus was perhaps not, as has been imagined, "a modest, unknown Alexandrian."[10] If, as we are justified in supposing, he already had contacts in the East with the senatorial aristocracy, it is not surprising to find him back at Rome, in close relations with such personages as Castricius Firmus, Marcellus Orontius, Sabillinus, and Rogatianus (V. P. 7, 24), all of whom belonged to this milieu.

As for Plotinian asceticism: there is nothing morbid or unhealthy about it. We find nothing in it which is not in conformity with that philosophical way of life which had, by the time of Plotinus, been traditional for centuries.

So Plotinus does not speak about his birth, his country, or his parents? He is simply putting into practice the advice of the Stoic Epictetus:

9. H/T/B Vol. Vc, pp. 84–85.
10. E. Bréhier, *Plotin: Les Ennéades*, p. vi.

If what the philosophers have said about the kinship between God and mankind is true, then what else remains for men but to imitate Socrates: when asked where he came from, he never said he was an Athenian or a Corinthian, but rather a citizen of the world. . . . Anyone who has familiarized himself with the administration of the world and learned that "what is greatest and lordly and all-inclusive of things is that system comprised of mankind and God, and it is from him that the seeds have come down, not just to my father and grandfather, but to everything that is born and grows upon the earth, especially to rational beings, since only they are suited by nature to commune with the society of God, being intertwined with him through reason"—why should he not call himself a citizen of the world? Why should he not call himself the son of god?[11]

Plotinus, we are told, "neglects the most elementary hygienic precautions." This is incorrect. It is not the case that Plotinus did not bother about the care and treatment of his body. He had his own qualified masseurs, probably slaves belonging to the household of Gemina, where he lived. It was no doubt in the private pool belonging to this house that he bathed, according to Roman custom, before being rubbed down. Plotinus did not, however, go to the *public* baths (*thermae*), simply because these establishments were places of amusement, dissipation, and pleasure. On this topic, one need only read Seneca's fifty-sixth *Letter,* which describes the deafening brouhaha resounding from a public bath near his home: the slapping of the masseurs' hands; the huffing and puffing of the gymnasts; the shouts of hawkers selling drinks and sausages; the yelping of the depilators and the shrieks of those undergoing their operations; the protests of thieves caught in the act; the shouts of tough guys looking for a fight. Plotinus was never able to resign himself to getting involved with such a tumult, even when his regular masseurs fell victim to the plague.

So he ate and slept little? Here again, there is nothing so extraordinary about that. Under the influence of Pythagoreanism, the custom of vegetarianism had long since become implanted. People contented themselves with a frugal regime, not out of asceticism, but for reasons of health. Plotinus himself recalls this fact, when he

11. Epictetus, *Discourses* I, 9, 1; 4–6. [The passage within quotation marks has been variously ascribed to Posidonius (Diogenes Laertius 7, 138) or to Chrysippus (Diels, *Doxographi Graeci,* pp. 464, 20; 465, 15).—Trans.]

attacks the Gnostics for pretending to cure diseases by exorcisms: "They say they can purify themselves of diseases; they would be right, if they said, as the philosophers do, that they do so by temperance and a well-ordered diet" (II 9, 14, 11–13).

With regard to sleep, Plato had already said that "too much sleep does no good either for the body or for the soul," and that we should "keep awake all the hours we can, only reserving for sleep what the body requires, and this is not much, when the habit has been well established."[12] In Plotinus' own entourage, there was a living example of the physical benefits procured by asceticism:

> Rogatianus was also a senator. He had advanced so far in the withdrawal from this kind of life that not only did he renounce all his possessions and send away all his slaves, but he also renounced his rank. When he was about to become praetor, and the lictors were waiting for him, he would not come out, nor did he show a care for his duties.[13] He no longer chose even to inhabit his own house, but used to go to some of his friends and acquaintances to eat and sleep there, although he took food only every other day. Indeed, such was his renunciation from, and lack of concern about, life that, whereas previously he had suffered so badly from gout that he had to be carried about on a chair, he recovered, and whereas before he had not been able to stretch forth his hands, he now used them with much greater dexterity than people who make their living with their hands. Plotinus took this man in and kept praising him as highly as he did anyone else and setting him forth as an example to philosophers. (V. P. 7, 31–46)

Finally, it seems difficult to say that Plotinus had a morbid complacency towards states of ill-health. Let us reread in its entirety the text to which Bréhier alluded:

12. Plato, *Laws* VII, 808b-c. [Cf. already Homer, *Iliad* 2, 24–25: "He should not sleep night long who is a man burdened with counsels/and responsibility for a people and cares so numerous."—Trans.]

13. [The praetorship was a highly honorific charge, praetors being responsible for justice at Rome. Upon their nomination, lictors—attendants/bodyguards who bore the *fasces,* a bundle of rods with an axe in the center—would march to the home of the new magistrate, where they would live throughout his term of office (H/T/B). As his first act of office, the new praetor would march, escorted by the lictors, from his home to the senate. Rogatianus' refusal to leave his house, even though the lictors were waiting for him, thus signified his refusal to participate in the ancient ritual of entry into the praetorship, and hence his refusal of the praetorship *tout court.*—Trans.]

The man of this world may be handsome, tall, and wealthy, and the leader of all men, inasmuch as he belongs to this place;[14] but he is not to be envied, for he is deceived by these things. As far as the sage is concerned, he may not even have these things to start with, but if he gets them he himself will diminish them, since he cares about *himself*. Moreover, he will cause *the body's excessive vitality* to wither and diminish through neglect, and will set aside offices. *Although taking care to maintain his health,* he will not wish to be totally without experience of illness, nor, of course, will he wish to be without experience of pain. Rather, even when they do not occur, he will wish to learn about them *while he is young.* When he is old, however, he will not wish to be obstructed by pains, pleasures, or by anything else pertaining to this world, be it pleasant or the reverse, so that he may not look towards the body. When he does enter into a painful situation, *he will oppose it with the power which has been provided for him against it,* but when he is experiencing pleasures, health, and lack of pain, he will not consider them an addition to his happiness, nor, when he is in the opposite condition, will he consider them a negation or diminution of it. If one condition does not add anything to a subject, how could the opposite condition take anything away from it? (I 4, 14, 14–32)

As we can see, Plotinus did not seek out sickness, suffering, or ugliness for their own sake. It is not the body he struggled against, but "the body's excessive vitality," which might throw the soul off balance in her flight towards the contemplation of the Good.[15] We must, he tells us, accustom ourselves not to pay attention to what the body feels, and to become indifferent both to pleasure and to pain, so as not to be distracted from contemplation. This means that we must accustom ourselves to "wish" for pain and suffering while we are still young, so that they will not take us by surprise when they come naturally, with old age.

We have here a spiritual exercise which was very familiar to the Stoics: that of "premeditation." Unpleasant events, they claimed, must be *willed in advance,* so that they may be borne more easily

14. [*Hôs an toude tou topou.* Cf. Plato, *Theaetetus* 176a: "Evils . . . have no place in the divine world, but they must haunt this mortal nature and this place (*tonde ton topon*) (H/T/B).—Trans.]

15. [On this point, see the sensitive analysis of Peter Brown, *The Body and Society,* New York: Columbia University Press, 1988, pp. 129–31 (on Plotinus' near-contemporary Clement of Alexandria).—Trans.]

when they occur at an inopportune moment. Freedom must keep one step ahead of that which threatens to constrain it.

One could easily find other examples in Plotinian asceticism of spiritual exercises held in esteem by the Stoics. Porphyry, for instance, tells us that Plotinus' "attention towards himself never let up for a moment" (V. P. 8, 20); and that "as long as he was awake, his inner tension never ceased" (ibid. 9, 17). By using these terms ("attention" = *prosochê*, "tension" = *tasis*), Porphyry is simply alluding to the technical vocabulary which designated vigilance, the fundamental attitude of the Stoic sage.

Plotinus' perpetual tension is thus no more unusual than that of Marcus Aurelius or Epictetus. But whereas the Stoic's attention was constantly directed towards the events of daily life, in which he tried always to recognize God's will, Plotinian attention was directed towards the Spirit. It was an ever-renewed effort to remain in a state of contemplation of the Good. One might therefore conclude that Plotinian attention turned away from reality and tried to escape it, taking refuge in abstraction, and that it consequently demanded more concentration and fatigue than the Stoic attitude.

Nothing could be further from the truth. In the wisdom of Plotinus, there is something gentle, smiling, benevolent: a sense of tact and a feel for reality that contrast sharply with the roughness and rigor of a Marcus Aurelius or an Epictetus. Before we can understand where this gentleness comes from, we must first be able to discern all its aspects.

□

Simplicity, breadth of spirit, benevolence, attentive sympathy: these are the keys to Plotinian pedagogy. "Anyone who so wished could attend his classes" (V. P. 1, 13).

Perhaps it was enough to draw aside the curtain which often, during this period, was the only thing separating the classroom from the street. Once inside, one could question the Master as much as one wished: "He used to encourage his listeners to ask questions themselves, and as a result his classes were full of disorder and idle babble, as Amelius told us" (V. P. 3, 35–38).

Such a procedure did not suit everyone's taste. Lovers of novelty and high-flown phrases were disappointed:

At that time, some people thought he was showing off by plagiarizing Numenius. They considered him a dull babbler, and held him in contempt, because they could not understand what he was saying. He kept himself pure of any sophistical grandstanding or affectation, and seemed rather to be engaging in conversation during his classes, so that the syllogistical necessity embodied within his reasonings was not immediately apparent to anybody. I, Porphyry, had the same impression when I first heard him. (V. P. 18, 2–10)

It was not long before Porphyry became one of Plotinus' favorite interlocutors, but this did not mollify his detractors. Quite the contrary:

A man, Thaumasius by name, entered the classroom, and declared that he wanted Plotinus to deal with general subjects, and that he should talk in such a way that what he said could be written down, because he could not stand these questions and answers exchanged between Plotinus and Porphyry. Plotinus replied, "But if we could not solve the problems Porphyry raises, we would be unable to say anything that could be written down."[16] (V. P. 13, 12–16)

This method of teaching, disconcerting as it was for some listeners, presupposed an unshakeable patience on Plotinus' part: "He

16. Another translation of this text has been suggested by M.-O. Goulet-Cazé, "L'arrière-plan scolaire de la *Vie de Plotin*," in L. Brisson et al. 1982, p. 268: "So, when a man by the name of Thaumasius came in, a high-ranking official of finances (*tous katholou logous prattontos*), who said that he wanted to hear him speak about texts (*eis biblia*) and that he could not stand Porphyry's questions and answers, Plotinus said: "But if we did not solve the difficulties raised by Porphyry's questions, we could say nothing whatsoever about the text." On this interpretation, the expression *katholou logous* does not mean "the general subjects" Thaumasius would like to hear Plotinus talk about, but rather "the accounts of the central government," and the participle *prattontos* would have as its subject not Plotinus, but Thaumasius (cf. A. H. M. Jones, J. R. Martindale and J. Morris, *The Prosopography of the Later Roman Empire,* Cambridge: Cambridge Univ. Press, 1971, p. 889). Moreover, on this interpretation the *biblia* are not collections of notes taken during the class, but texts to be commented on *during* the class; cf. O. Schissel, "Der Stundenplan des Neuplatonikers Proklos," *Byzantinische Zeitschrift* 26 (1926), pp. 266–169). Within the limits of this work, I cannot deal with the complex questions raised by the interpretation of this text. I shall return to it elsewhere. In any case, we have here a good example of the difficulties often involved in the exegesis and translation of texts from Antiquity. On the idiom *eis biblia* ("on texts"), one may note an analogous turn of phrase in Plutarch, *An seni sit gerenda respublica,* 796c: *scholas epi bibliois perainontas,* "conducting their classes on texts."

showed his gentle tolerance for questions as well as his vigor in answering them; for instance, when I, Porphyry, questioned him for three days on how the soul is present in the body, he continued demonstrating his teachings to me without a break" (V. P. 13, 9–12).

It was not always the audience who asked the questions. Sometimes a student would read a commentary by one of the great exegetes of the second and third centuries A.D., Alexander or Numenius, for instance, on a text from Plato or Aristotle. Then Plotinus would speak. "Plotinus borrowed nothing at all from these commentaries; on the contrary, he was personal and original in his theoretical reflection, and brought to his investigations the spirit of Ammonius. . . . He would explain the meaning of a profound doctrine in a few words, and then stand up to leave"[17] (V. P. 14, 14–18).

Plotinus went straight to the heart of the matter; his contemplation was never interrupted, and he did not bother about literary style. Yet his passion for the subject in which he was absorbed gave him a natural eloquence:

In his classes, he was a gifted speaker, and was extremely good at inventing and coming up with appropriate points, but he did make some mistakes in the pronunciation of certain words . . . which also crept into his writing. His intelligence was clearly evident when he spoke; its light used to illuminate his face. He was always pleasant to look at, but in those moments he was even more beautiful. He would break into a light sweat, and his gentleness shone forth. (V. P. 13, 1–8)

In the following anecdote, there is probably a trace of modesty, or even timidity:[18] "One day, when Origen came into his class, Plotinus blushed from head to toe, and made as if to stand up and put an end to the class. When Origen urged him to continue, Plotinus said: "One's desire to talk is reduced when one knows that one is about to speak to people who already know what he is going to say"[19] (V. P. 14, 20–24).

17. Translation based on that of M.-O. Goulet-Cazé, *loc. cit.*, pp. 262–63.
18. One might also suppose that Plotinus, who "brought the spirit of Ammonius into his investigations," thought he had nothing to teach to a former classmate from Ammonius' school.
19. [This Origen is not, of course, the Christian Church Father, but the pagan Neoplatonist philosopher, Plotinus' fellow student at the school of Ammonius.— Trans.]

Be that as it may, Plotinus recommended simplicity and modesty to his disciples. "The kind of philosophy we pursue is characterized—apart from all its other positive effects—by simplicity of character and pure thinking. It pursues what is venerable, not what is arrogant; and if it inclines towards boldness, it is not without reason, a great deal of assurance, caution, and the greatest circumspection" (II 9, 14, 38–43).

In all this, we can recognize the same disdain for the merely external, the same intent not to try to impress by arrogant or affected appearances. Plotinus did not want to abuse the prestige of form, to seduce, or to force agreement. We find the same attitude in his style of writing:

> In his writing he was concise, clever, and brief, and more abundant in thoughts than he was in words. He usually wrote in a state of inspiration and passionate intensity (V. P. 14, 1–3). . . . Once he had written something, he never managed to revise his text by going over it a second time. What is more, he never even managed to read it and get through it to the end, because his sight did not help him enough to be able to read.[20] He did not form his letters in an attractive way, nor did he separate his syllables distinctly, nor was he concerned about orthography: he cared only about the meaning. Moreover—and this used to astonish us all—he stuck to this style of writing right to the end of his life. (V. P. 8, 1–8)

His books were the product of intense meditation:

> He used to complete his theoretical inquiries within himself, from beginning to end, and then commit the results of his reflections to writing, and string them together, writing down what he had stored up in his soul in such a way that he seemed to be copying straight out of a book. Even when talking with someone, and carrying on a conversation, his attention was still fixed on his reflections, so that he was able, at the same time, to fulfill the obligations of conversation and maintain his faculty of discursive thought directed uninterruptedly towards the matters under investigation. When his interlocutor left, he did not take up again what he had written down—as we have said, his eyesight was not good enough for him to take something up again—he would pick up where he left off, as if no time had elapsed from

20. In the translation of this passage, I have taken into account the long and interesting study that D. O'Brien has devoted to this text (L. Brisson et al., 1982, pp. 331–67), but without adopting all of his conclusions. I have modified the version given by O'Brien (*loc. cit.,* p. 360) on several points.

the time when he was carrying out the conversation. Thus, he was simultaneously present both to himself and to others. (V. P. 8, 8–20)

What an admirable formula, and how admirably it sums up Plotinus' entire secret!

No doubt, this was an extraordinary gift on Plotinus' part, as his disciples were well aware. Yet there is a sense in which this extraordinary strength of spirit seems to proceed from a moral requirement. Plotinus refused to stop contemplating, but at the same time he would not refuse himself to others. It is as though the complete receptivity in which he established himself with regard to God allowed him, and even commanded him, also to remain in a state of complete receptivity and availability with regard to other people.

□

In his capacity as spiritual guide, Plotinus maintained his benevolence, gentleness, and respect for others.

He took care personally to supervise his disciples' work. For example, Amelius was charged with writing a response to Porphyry, who, as a newcomer to the school, had difficulty in accepting one of the important points of Plotinus' teaching (V. P. 18, 10–19). We should also recall the incident involving the rhetorician Diophanes: Plotinus, scandalized by the latter's defense of Alcibiades, asked Porphyry to write a refutation (V. P. 15, 7–18). Similarly, Porphyry was requested to make a report to Plotinus on some philosophical treatises that Euboulos, an Athenian philosopher, had sent to his master (V. P. 15, 18–22). In the course of his attack on the Gnostics, Plotinus refuted the essential tenets of their doctrine in his classes and in a treatise, but left to Amelius and Porphyry the task of examining and discussing the totality of their writings (V. P. 16, 9–20). To this we must add the notes his students took during his classes (V. P. 3, 46–49), and the fact that he entrusted to his students the revision of the treatises which he himself had composed (V. P. 7, 50–52).

Not without vanity, Porphyry emphasizes the kind encouragement he received from his master, and in so doing, he gives us a rather lively picture of the life of the school:

Plotinus . . . used to sacrifice on the traditional birthdays of Plato and Socrates, and offer a feast for his companions, on which occasion those of them who were able had to read a speech before the guests (V. P. 2, 40–44). . . . Once, during the Plato celebrations, I read a poem entitled "The Sacred Marriage." Since much of what I said was, because of its mystical nature, said in an inspired and veiled way, someone said, "Porphyry has gone crazy!" But Plotinus said, loud enough for everyone to hear, "You have shown yourself a poet, a philosopher, and a hierophant."[21] (V. P. 15, 1–6)

We have already encountered the anecdote in which Plotinus repeated throughout a speech by Porphyry the Homeric verse "Strike thus, if you would become a light for men" (V. P. 15, 15), or replied to Thaumasius: "If Porphyry did not ask me questions, I would have nothing to say that could be written down"[22] (V. P. 13, 15).

Behind Porphyry's anxiousness to show off, we can surmise the internal rivalries at the school, and particularly the jealousy Porphyry felt towards Amelius, who, when Porphyry arrived at Rome, had already known Plotinus for eighteen years. These are phenomena common enough in every kind of school, be it spiritual or philosophical. It does seem, however, that Plotinus did not show any preferences. He accepted each student for what he was, and tried to get each one to develop what was best within him.

It has often been said that Plotinus lived within a narrow, confined circle. Joseph Bidez speaks of a "conventicule," "a little cenacle of pale, cloistered people."[23] For his part, Dr. Gillet discerns, in the preference Plotinus accorded to the closed group of his disciples, the symptom of a nervous disposition linked with tuberculosis.

Here again, however, Porphyry's account has been wrongly interpreted. He distinguishes between Plotinus' numerous auditors, on the one hand, and on the other the restricted group of adepts (V. P. 7, 1). This distinction can, however, be made with regard to any philosophical school of Antiquity, and especially of Late Antiquity. We must not think of the philosopher of this period on the model of a university professor, giving public classes. As we remarked above, he was a spiritual guide. Some people came to hear him but did not undergo a conversion. Others changed their lives completely, enter-

21. [A *hierophant* was the priest who presided over the Eleusinian Mysteries. Literally "shower/displayer of sacred things", he revealed the meaning of the Mysteries to the initiates.—Trans.]

22. Cf. above, pp. 53; 83.

23. Joseph Bidez, *Vie de Porphyre*, Gand, 1913, p. 39.

ing his school, receiving his advice, and wishing to live close to him. They became his companions (*hetairoi,* V. P. 2, 42), but also his adepts (*zêlôtai,* V. P. 7, 1). It was not a doctrine that these latter were adopting, but a way of life. The disciples of Musonius Rufus and Epictetus had done likewise, one hundred years previously.[24]

Porphyry also informs us that Plotinus' writings were available only to his adepts: "These books were entrusted only to a small number of persons, for it was not yet easy to obtain them; they were given out with a bad conscience, and not simply or recklessly. Rather, every effort was made to choose those who were to receive them" (V. P. 4, 14–17).

Porphyry himself was not given access to them until he had proved he had a good understanding of the Master's thought. After hearing Plotinus for the first time, he had written a tractate to argue a doctrinal point[25] which he could not accept:

> Plotinus had Amelius read what I had written, and when he had finished reading, Plotinus smiled and said, "It's up to you, Amelius, to solve the problems into which Porphyry has fallen out of ignorance of our views." Amelius then wrote a rather lengthy book entitled "Against the Objections of Porphyry." I in turn wrote a response to this, and Amelius replied to my writing. On the third time, I, Porphyry, was able—albeit with difficulty—to understand what was being said, and I changed my views, whereupon I wrote a retraction, which I read before the assembly. From that time on, I was given access to Plotinus' text.

In order to understand Porphyry's meaning, we must recall what it meant to publish a book in Antiquity. We must bear in mind that literary production, at that time, took the form of manuscripts, which could be recopied and falsified at will.[26] To publish a book

24. [Musonius Rufus (c. 30–101 A.D.) was the Stoic teacher of Epictetus (c. 55–135 A.D.). The *Discourses* and *Manual* of Epictetus, as transcribed by his student Arrian of Nicomedia, are among our most important sources on Stoicism.—Trans.]

25. [The doctrinal point was about whether the Intelligibles, or Platonic Forms, existed within or outside the hypostasis Intellect. Porphyry, like his teacher Longinus of Athens, was initially of the latter opinion; Plotinus devoted an entire treatise of the *Enneads* (V 5) to defending the former view.—Trans.]

26. On the publication of books in Antiquity, see E. Arns, *La technique du livre d'après saint Jérôme,* pp. 81–89; and M.-O. Goulet-Cazé, in L. Brisson et al., 1982, pp. 284–87 and the literature cited at p. 285, n. 2.

almost always meant to entrust it to a circle of friends, who undertook to insure its circulation as they deemed fit. For a philosopher,
this circle of friends was obviously the group of his true disciples:
those who had understood his true doctrine. Only they were capable
of attesting to the authenticity of his works, having them copied, and
making them known. Besides, the philosopher was not writing for
all of humanity, or a universal audience. It would be more accurate
to say that he was responding in writing to the questions raised by
his disciples. Such literary productions, arising out of particular circumstances, were addressed to a particular audience, if not to one
single individual: "Plotinus had begun to write on whatever topics
arose (V. P. 4, 10–11). Many investigations were undertaken in
our meetings with him, and Amelius and I urged him to set them
down in writing (ibid., 5, 5–7). . . . He took the subjects [sc. of his
treatises] from the problems which happened to come up" (ibid.,
5, 60–61).

Thus, Plotinus' small group of disciples were at the same time
the guardians and the addressees of the Master's writings. When
Plotinus took care to see that his writings were not handed over to
just anyone, he was only conforming to a widespread practice; it is
not, moreover, difficult to understand the need for it. One of the let-
ters of Saint Augustine, for example, gives a list of the friends to
whom one of his writings may be given.[27]

Porphyry's reason for insisting on this point is that he wanted to
emphasize for his readers his own importance within the school.
Not only had Plotinus allowed his writings to be given to him—
already a considerable privilege—but he had entrusted him with re-
vising and preparing a definitive edition of them. We may note in
passing here Plotinus' wisdom as a spiritual guide: Porphyry was a
good philologist, so he had to be given the chance to put into practice his own particular talent.

As a matter of fact, even during Plotinus' lifetime, the diffusion of
his writings had reached well beyond the circle of his immediate disciples. For instance, we find Porphyry's former teacher, the Athenian
philosopher and rhetorician Longinus—by no means a convert to

27. Henri-Irénée Marrou, "La technique de l'édition à l'époque patristique," *Vigi-
liae Christianae* 3 (1949), p. 217.

Plotinus' ideas—writing to Porphyry to ask him to send him some of our philosopher's treatises, to be added to the ones Amelius had already procured for him (V. P. 19, 6).

We cannot therefore conclude, from the mere fact that Plotinus kept watch over the distribution of his treatises, that he must have lived in the rarified atmosphere of a tiny cenacle.

If, moreover, we read carefully the list of Plotinus' adepts transmitted to us by Porphyry, we shall realize that the group was made up of very different personalities. Many of Plotinus' friends, even among his closest, were not genuine converts to philosophy. Even the distinction between auditors and adepts was not always very clearly drawn:[28]

> He had many auditors. As for genuine adepts, however, who had come together out of love for philosophy, there was first of all Amelius of Etruria, whose family name was Gentilianus. Plotinus preferred to call him *Amerius* (with an "*r*"), because, he said, it was better for him to derive his name from *amereia* ("indivisibility") than from *ameleia* ("negligence"). There was also a doctor, Paulinus of Scythopolis, whom Amelius used to call "tiny" (*mikkalos*). He had a great deal of poorly digested knowledge. Another of Plotinus' disciples was Eustochius, a doctor from Alexandria. Plotinus met him near the end of his life, and remained under his care until his death. Eustochius devoted himself entirely to Plotinus' teachings and reached the state of a genuine philosopher. There was also Zoticus, the critic and poet who had revised the works of Antimachus and set Plato's *Critias* to some very fine verse. He, however, lost his sight, and died not long before Plotinus. Another of Plotinus' companions was Zethus, of Arabian origin, who was married to the daughter of Theodosius, a companion of Ammonius. He, too, was a doctor, and Plotinus was very fond of him. He was a politician, and had a strong penchant—which Plotinus tried to restrain—for politics. Plotinus was on such intimate terms with him that he retired to his country estate, six miles from Minturna. (V. P. 7, 1–23)

There follows a list of the politicians, especially senators, who were Plotinus' auditors: Castricius Firmus, Marcellus Orontius, Sabinillus, and Rogatianus, with whose story we are already familiar. Then comes another Egyptian: "Three was also Serapion of Alexandria, a former rhetorician, who later was present at the philo-

28. On the individuals mentioned in the *Life of Plotinus*, see L. Brisson, *Prosopographie,* in L. Brisson et al., 1982, pp. 56–114.

sophical discussions. He was, however, not able to refrain from the bad habit of money matters and lending out money at interest" (V. P. 7, 46–49).

And finally: "He also counted me, Porphyry of Tyre, amongst his closest companions, and he chose to entrust to me the correction of his writings" (V. P. 7, 49–51).

We thus discover a highly variegated milieu: it contained genuine philosophers but also doctors, philologists, politicians, and usurers. Plotinus' friendship was not necessarily bestowed on the best practitioners of his philosophy. Zethus, for instance, who had not completely detached himself from political concerns, was still on very friendly terms with him.

No, Plotinus did not live amidst "pale and cloistered people." The house where he lived probably resounded with bursts of laughter, games, and shouting. It was certainly quite large, since it was owned by Gemina, a woman who belonged, it would seem, to the Roman aristocracy. There, Plotinus was far from being alone. "Many men and women of the most eminent families, when they were about to die, brought their children to Plotinus—males as well as females— and handed them over to him, along with all their possessions, as if to a kind of holy and divine guardian. This was why his house had become full of boys and girls" (V. P. 9, 5–10).

Porphyry points out the special care Plotinus lavished on his wards: "One of these children was Potamon; Plotinus directed his education and often listened to him recite his school exercises" (V. P. 9, 10–11).

This role as a guardian involved Plotinus in a multitude of accounting duties. "He did not shrink from examining the accounts given to him by the people responsible for the well-being of these children, and he was careful to insure their exactitude. He used to say that, as they were too young to be philosophers, their revenues and possessions had to be kept intact and untouched" (V. P. 9, 12–16).

There were also domestic incidents. "One day, Chione, a widow who, along with her children, led a dignified life in Plotinus' home, had a valuable necklace stolen. When all the slaves were brought before Plotinus, he pointed to one of them and said, 'That one is the thief.' The slave was flogged, and denied it at first; but he finally confessed, brought back what he had stolen, and returned the necklace to its rightful owner" (V. P. 11, 2–8). As Porphyry rightly comments, apropos of this story, "Such was the abundance of Plotinus' understanding of character" (V. P. 11, 1).

Plotinus finds his man through the eyes. Here again, we encounter the theme of vision. "One could know a man's character by looking him in the eyes, or by observing some other parts of his body. There we can read the dangers threatening him, and his possible means of salvation (II 3, 7, 9–10).

Plotinus' vision, before which everything opens up, is a vision which comes from beyond and penetrates, behind appearances, as far as spiritual reality. This is the mode of vision of souls in the intelligible world: "Even in this world, we know a great deal about people even when they are silent, through their eyes. There [i.e. in the intelligible world], however, the whole body is pure, and each person is like an eye; there is nothing hidden or fabricated, but before one person speaks to another, the latter has already understood just by looking at him" (IV 3, 18, 19–22).

We find Plotinus applying his spiritual vision to the people around him. "He could predict what would become of each of the children who lived with him. He predicted, for instance, that Polemon would be a lover and would not live long; and this is what happened" (V. P. 11, 8–11). Porphyry himself experienced his spiritual insight: "Once, he sensed that I, Porphyry, was considering killing myself. He suddenly came up to me, when I was living in his house, and told me that my desire did not come from a spiritual condition, but from some kind of melancholic illness, and he ordered me to go abroad. I was persuaded by him, and left for Sicily. . . I gave up my desire, and was prevented from being with Plotinus up until his death" (V. P. 11, 11–19).

What a precious anecdote! The disciple was going through a very serious spiritual crisis: Plotinus keeps on saying that we must separate ourselves from our bodies; so why not do it physically and voluntarily, once and for all? Why not get away from here, when one is tired of the body and of life? Didn't the Stoics say that the wise man is free to leave this world when he so wishes? What a surprise, however, while rehashing these dark thoughts, to see Plotinus heading towards you and saying: "What you are planning does not come

from the Spirit, but from the body. It's the result of an abnormal condition of the bile!" What a surprise, to be seen through right down
to your inner recesses, and to discover that "that's all it is"; what a
surprise, finally, to hear such a simple remedy suggested! And yet,
this remedy turns your whole life upside down. For six years, you
had been trying to hold down first place in the school, making a continuous effort of intense research, asceticism, and meditation. And
now the teacher comes along and sends you away, "to get some fresh
air."

What depth, delicacy, and good sense in Plotinus' spiritual direction! Not only was he able to guess Porphyry's inner crisis, but he
understood its true significance. Porphyry sincerely believed himself to be moved by the Spirit. Plotinus, however, saw right away that
it was nothing of the sort, and yet he knew just as well that Porphyry
was not responsible for his condition. It was an illness, and had to be
treated as such. The remedy would be simple enough: get a change
of scenery, travel. And yet, Porphyry no doubt derived a spiritual
benefit from his voyage: he found himself again, far from the feverish
climate of Rome and the rivalries and ambitions which were perhaps
the real cause of his melancholy.

Plotinus was thus no sage, hiding in an ivory tower. In Gemina's
house, there were orphans, Chione and her children, thieving
slaves, and disciples who sometimes went through dramatic psychological crises.

And yet, although he was responsible for the cares and concerns of the
lives of so many people, he never—as long as he was awake—let slacken his
constant tension directed towards the Spirit. He was gentle, and always at
the disposition of everyone who had any kind of relationship with him. This
was why, although he spent twenty-six entire years in Rome, and acted as
arbitrator in disputes between many people, he never made a single enemy
amongst the politicians. (V. P. 9, 16–22)

□

Plotinus' gentleness was a conscious spiritual attitude which presupposed all of his spiritual experience.

We must, he taught, accept the sensible world, because it is the
manifestation of the world of Forms.

Perhaps the Gnostics will say that their doctrine causes us to flee from the body, and to hate it from a distance, whereas ours attaches the soul to the body. But it is as if two people were living in the same well-built house: one of them criticizes its structure and its builder, although he keeps on living in it all the same. The other, however, does not criticize; in fact, he affirms the builder has constructed the house with consummate skill, and he awaits the time when he will move on, and no longer have need of a house (II 9, 18, 1–9). He who finds fault with the nature of the universe does not know what he is doing, nor how far his arrogance is taking him. The reason is that they do not know about the successive order of things, from the first to the second to the third and down to the last things; nor do they know that we must not abuse those things which are lower than the first, but gently acquiesce in the nature of all things. (V. P. II 9, 13, 1–6)

We must accept our own bodies with gentleness. The sage knows that he needs only to gather himself together,[29] in order for the lower part of himself to become calm, and leave him to his contemplation. If, however, the body comes to bother him again, he will put up with it patiently:

In order for the soul to separate herself from the body, perhaps it is necessary for her to gather herself up into herself from what, for her, corresponds to the places she has been in; at any rate she must remain free of passions. As for inevitable pleasures, she must, in order not to be hindered, turn them into mere sensations: processes of healing and of relief from pain. Pain is to be eliminated, or, if this is impossible, is to be borne *with gentleness,* and diminished by not suffering along with it. (I 2, 5, 5–11)

Plotinus goes on to specify how the soul must remain independent of her inferior part, whose faculties—desire and aggressivity—can disturb the body. He then continues, "In short, the soul herself will be pure from all these things, and will wish to make her irrational part pure from them as well. In this way she will not be disturbed,[30] or if at all, then not intensely; but the disturbances will be

29. [*Se recueillir.* See above, chap. 5, p. 65 n. 2.—Trans.]
30. [*Plêtessthai.* The image comes from the world of music: *plêtessthai* is what happens to a string when it is plucked (H/T/B). The prephilosophical soul is thus pictured as a tightly strung cord, caused to twang violently by every outside emotion.—Trans.]

few and easily dissolved by the proximity [sc. of the Spirit]" (I, 2, 5, 21–24).

The profound meaning of this gentleness towards oneself is given in the following lines: "It is as if a person were living next door to a sage and derived the benefits of his vicinity: either he becomes like the sage, or else he is so ashamed as not to dare to do anything the good man would disapprove. *Thus there will no longer be a conflict,* since the lower part respects the rational soul; *when Reason is present, it is enough,* to the point that the irrational part itself is disgusted if it is stirred at all and does not keep its peace in the presence of its Master, and it reproaches itself with weakness" (I 2, 5, 25–31).

We are here getting close to the secret of Plotinian gentleness. By the mere presence of his spiritual life, the sage transforms both the lower part of himself and the people who come in contact with him. From one end of reality to the other, the most effective mode of action is pure presence. The Good acts on the Spirit by its mere presence; the Spirit acts on the soul, and the soul on the body; all by their presence alone.

There is thus no struggle against the self, no spiritual "combat" in Plotinian asceticism. It is enough that the soul contemplate, turning herself towards God, for all of being—down to its most inferior components—to be transformed.

One might think that this contemplation absorbs the soul and prevents her from paying attention to external things. But Plotinus' life is testimony to the fact that once a specific degree of inner purity is attained, when contemplation has become continuous, and vision has been purified and become as if luminous, attention paid to the Spirit does not exclude attention to other people, to the world, and to the body itself. It is by means of the same availability, the same loving attendance, that we can be present at the same time to the Spirit and to other people. Such attention is mildness and gentleness. Once transformed, our vision perceives, shining on all things, the grace that makes God manifest. Plotinus' vision, established in the Good, sees, as it were, all things being born from the Good. Then there is no longer an outside and an inside: only one single light, towards which the soul feels only gentleness: "The better one is, the more kind he is towards all things and towards mankind" (II 9, 9, 44–45).

Plotinus' entire life consisted in the experience that gentleness, like grace, proclaims the presence of the Principle of all things: "The Good is gentle, mild, and very delicate, and always at the disposition of whomever desires it" (V 5, 12, 33–35).

VII

Solitude

> To flee alone, towards the Solitary One.
>
> (VI 9, 11, 50)

There was a dream in Plotinus' life—a dream with the slightly pompous but evocative name of Platonopolis:[1]

The Emperor Gallienus and his wife Salonina held Plotinus in esteem and veneration. Taking advantage of their friendship, Plotinus thus decided to re-establish a city of philosophers[2] which was said to have existed in Campania but which now, at any rate, lay in ruins. Once the city was inhabited, the surrounding territory was to be attributed to it, and those who went to live there were to live according to the laws of Plato. It was to be called Platonopolis, and Plotinus undertook that he himself would move there, along with his companions. Moreover, the Philosopher would easily have had his wish fulfilled, were it not that some members of the Emperor's entourage put obstacles in his way, whether out of jealousy, ill-will, or some other base motive." (V. P. 12, 1–12)

What were the real reasons for this fiasco? Did Gallienus' advisers immediately understand that Plotinus "did not have the makings of a founder of cities"?[3] Did the emperor himself wish to make clear in this way his hostility to the senatorial milieu, which tended to gravitate around Plotinus, and which might have found a territorial foothold in the new Platonic city?[4]

In any event, this story remains highly enigmatic. It is difficult to know exactly what Plotinus had in mind. It has been said that "Platonopolis is the Platonic city changed into a convent."[5] No doubt

1. On Platonopolis, see the bibliography by L. Brisson in L. Brisson et al., 1982, pp. 121–22.
2. R. Harder, in *Porphyrius, Über Plotins Leben,* Hamburg, 1958, p. 104, puts forth some rather forceful arguments against this manuscript reading.
3. Emile Bréhier, *Plotin, Les Ennéades,* vol. 1, p. xiii.
4. R. Harder, *Plotins Schriften,* vol. Vc, p. 321.
5. E. Bréhier, *Plotin, Les Ennéades,* vol. 1, p. xiii.

this is true, and for this period there is nothing extraordinary about it. Such convent-like communities had already been in existence for centuries, and they seemed to offer the ideal conditions for leading a philosophical life. There had been Pythagorean communities, for example, and convents of the Essenes. In general, the idea of a completely contemplative life of studious leisure, whose pleasantness would be still further enhanced by the pure pleasure of spiritual friendship, exerted on all of Antiquity a fascination which seemed only to increase at the end of the Roman Empire. One hundred years after Plotinus, Augustine, too, before his conversion, would dream of a phalanstery[6] of philosophers, where, in leisure and complete communal ownership of possessions, he and his friends could "flee the noise and annoyances of human life."[7] To some extent, he would later realize this dream on Verecundus' property at Cassiacum.[8] But the astonishing aspect of Plotinus' project is its dimensions. We are not talking about a tiny community, but about an entire city, whose inhabitants were to live according to the laws of Plato. When one thinks of Plotinus' hostility to all forms of political activity, such a project is all the more astonishing. We have no choice but to believe that Plotinus, who makes almost no allusions to Plato's politics in his writings, wanted to put the political part of Plato's teaching into practice. No doubt, he conceived of this politics as the organization of a life entirely devoted to contemplation. For him, the sage could—but was not obliged to—consider engaging in this kind of activity:

Once one has been united to him, and has had, as it were, sufficient communion with him, *then*—if he can—let him go and announce to someone else what union is like in that other world. It was because he carried out

6. [*Phalanstère*. In the scheme of the French socialist Charles Fourier (1772–1837), society was to be divided into a series of "phalanstères" (from "phalanx" and "monastery"); that is, groups harmoniously composed with a view to procuring well-being for each member, on the basis of enjoyable, freely contracted labor.—Trans.]

7. Augustine, *Confessions,* book VI, 14, 24.

8. [In September 386 A.D., shortly after his conversion to Christianity, Augustine retired to the estate of the Milanese professor Verecundus at Cassiacum (perhaps the modern Cassago in Brianza), where he embarked on a period of scholarly leisure. Cf. Peter Brown, *Augustine of Hippo: A Biography,* London: Faber and Faber, 1967, chap. 11.—Trans.]

such a union that Minos was reported to be the "close companion of Zeus,"[9] and when he recalled that union, it was as images of it that he used to lay down his laws; so filled was he by contact with the divine that he was able to legislate. Alternatively, if one feels that political activities are beneath him, let him remain up above, if he so desires. (VI 9, 7, 21–27)

Although it is difficult to guess how Platonopolis might have turned out, we may at least suppose that Plotinus imagined, when he dreamed this dream, that philosophy would be able to diffuse its influence over a large number of people and that a community, large enough so that Plato's *Republic* could be put into practice in it, would group itself around him.[10]

It is thus all the more poignant to watch Plotinus, as he nears the end of his life, sinking into solitude and suffering.

At the beginning of the year 268, Plotinus himself had advised Porphyry to leave him and go traveling.[11] In the same or the following year, Amelius left him too, in order to join Longinus at the court of Queen Zenobia in Phoenician Tyre.[12] Plotinus' favorite students were thus far away from him, and this was the moment when he was struck down by illness.

9. [At Homer, *Odyssey* 19, 178–79, Minos is called *Dios megalou oaristês.* Modern scholars disagree as to the meaning of *oaristês,* but Plotinus, following the commentary on this verse in the Pseudo-Platonic *Minos* 318eff., understands it as meaning "close companion." Minos, legendary King of Crete, builder of the Labyrinth at Cnossos, and stepfather of the Minotaur, also had the reputation of being a great lawgiver. In the *Minos,* we learn that the great king used to ascend every nine years into the cave of Zeus to receive instruction, and that it was from these brainstorming sessions that he derived those laws "in which Crete has always rejoiced, as does Sparta, since she recognized them as divine and started to use them." (Pseudo-Plato, *Minos* 320b). Plotinus' mystical/sexual interpretation of the tale, in which Minos is filled— one might almost translate "impregnated"—with his laws while in a state of contact with Zeus, seems to be entirely his own, and was to exercise great influence on Western mysticism (H/T/B).—Trans.]

10. In his text, Plotinus does not speak about Plato's *Republic,* but about Plato's "laws"; we should probably read "Laws" with a capital "L", for Plotinus probably had in mind the organization of a city as it is described in Plato's dialogue *The Laws.*

11. It is possible that the dispersion of Plotinus' school in 269 may have been linked to the assassination of the emperor Gallienus, who had been friendly towards Plotinus and his disciples. See M. Wundt, *Plotin,* Leipzig, 1919, p. 45.

12. Cf. L. Brisson, "Amelius," in *Aufstieg und Niedergang der römischen Welt,* part II, vol. 36, 2 (1987), p. 800.

In a short time, a fierce case of quinsy[13] had set in. As long as I was present, he still showed no sign of his illness, but once I had sailed away it become chronic, as I heard the story upon my return from Plotinus' companion Eustochios, who had stayed with him until his death. His voice lost its clear, melodious tone as he became hoarse, his vision was blurred, and he developed ulcerous sores on his hands and feet. Since he had the custom of greeting all his friends with a kiss, they began to avoid his company; he therefore left the City and took up residence on the property of Zethus, a former old companion of his who had now died. There, the necessities of life were supplied to him from the possessions of Zethus and were also brought to him from Castricius' holdings in Minturnae, since it was in Minturnae that Castricius had his property. . . . Eustochius was living in Puteoli.[14] (V. P. 2, 9–25)

What exactly was the nature of Plotinus' illness? Were the symptoms diagnosed by Eustochius those of *elephantiasis graeca,* or tuberculous leprosy, as Oppermann thought,[15] or of pulmonary tuberculosis, as Dr. Gillet believed? The question is hard to resolve. In any case, the disease was so repulsive that all the Master's friends and disciples fled from him. Thereupon, he withdrew to Zethus' estate, where in the past he had often spent the summer holidays.

Reading this story, one thinks of the terrible *pensée* of Pascal: "It is certainly very pleasant to relax in the company of our fellows! But they are as miserable and impotent as we are; they won't help us. We shall die alone. Therefore, we must act as if we were alone."[16]

Both in Rome, as he watched his disciples leave him, and later in

13. [*Kunanchou.* Porphyry mentions this same illness in his *On Abstinence* 3, 7 (eds. J. Bouffartigue and M. Patillon, Paris: Les Belles Lettres, 1979, vol. 2, p. 161). I have rendered these editors' "esquinancie" (note 3, p. 237) by the more current "quinsy," which has the merit of preserving its etymological derivation from the Greek *kunanchou* (lit. "dog-choker"). The OED defines quinsy as "inflammation of the throat . . . suppuration of the tonsils." Alexander of Tralles, *Therapeutica* (ed. T. Putschmann, Vienna, 1878, vol. 2, p. 125, 24–25), writing in the sixth century A.D., defines *kunanchê* as an "inner inflammation of the muscles of the larynx."— Trans.]

14. [Minturnae was a town near the sea in Campania, just north of Naples and some 100 miles southwest of Rome, while Puteoli—the modern Pouzzoli—was some fifty miles further to the southwest.—Trans.]

15. H. Oppermann, *Plotins Leben,* Heidelberg, 1929.

16. Pascal, *pensée* no. 211 Brunschvicg.

Campania, Plotinus kept on writing. From this point on, his trea
tises deal only with ethical subjects: wisdom, happiness, Providence, the origin of evil, death. He sent them to Porphyry, but it is as
if he were writing only for himself. They are his last soliloquies.
Their abstract, impersonal form cannot completely hide the effort
Plotinus was making to attain serenity. He painted for himself a portrait of the ideal sage:

Being happy pertains only to that which has an excess of life. . . . Perfect,
true, and genuine life consists in that intellective nature. . . . The other
kinds are incomplete; mere images of life, their mode of existence is neither
perfect nor pure. . . . That person's life is complete who possesses not only
the faculty of sensation, but also rationality and true Spirit. . . . The person
who is happy here and now [is] the one who *is* this form of life in actuality,
and has reached the stage of becoming this life itself. At this point, other
things merely act as a surrounding medium for him. One could not say that
they were a part of him, since he does not want them to be surrounding him;
only if they were joined to him through an act of his will could they be said
to belong to him. For someone like that, then, what is the Good? He is his
own good for himself, thanks to what he possesses. The cause of the Good
within him is the transcendent Good. . . . The person in this state no longer
seeks anything; for what could he seek? Certainly not for anything inferior
to him; and, as for what is best, he is with it already. (I 4, 3, 24–4, 23)[17]

The sage accustoms himself to looking at things *sub specie aeter-
nitatis:*[18]

What is there in human affairs so great that it will not be despised by the
person who has risen above them, and who is no longer dependent on anything here down below? Such a person will not consider even the greatest
strokes of good luck to be of importance, whether they be ruling over king-
doms, power over cities and peoples, or colonizations and foundations of
cities, even if he is responsible for them himself. Will such a person, then,
think it important if he is thrown out of power, or if he sees his own city
razed to the ground? . . . He would no longer be a sage if he considered that
wood and stones were important; nor, for that matter, that mortal beings

17. Saint Ambrose utilized this entire treatise in his sermon *De Jacob et vita beata*
["On Jacob and the Blessed Life"—Trans.]. With the present passage, compare *On
Jacob* 1, 7, 29.
18. ["From the point of view of eternity."—Trans.]

should die! After all, we say that such a person should believe that death is better than life with the body.[19] (I 4, 7, 14–26)

During this period, Plotinus abundantly developed a theme which had been traditional since the Stoics: suffering, disease, and disasters have no effect on the sage, because he remains independent with regard to external circumstances. "As for his own sufferings: when they are intense, he will bear them as long as he is able; but if they become too strong, they will carry him away. Nor will he be pitiable in his suffering, for his inner flame still burns as does the light within a lantern, though outside there rage the fierce winds of a winter storm" (I 4, 8, 1–6).[20]

The image of the lyre will help us to understand Plotinus' attitude of inner freedom:

The sage will care for his earthly self and put up with it as long as he can, as a musician does with his lyre, as long as it is still serviceable. When it is not, he will exchange it for another, or else he will abandon his lyre and will give up playing on the lyre altogether, since he now has another task to perform, without a lyre. He will leave it lying next to him and keep on singing, now without an instrument. Yet it was not in vain that the instrument was given to him in the first place, for he has played on it many a time.[21] (I 4, 16, 22–29)

Another traditional image. But how personal is the final line! How well it expresses Plotinus' fundamental gentleness! He shows no trace of irritation against the body which is making him suffer, which is now useless, and which he will soon dispose of. Soon it will

19. Augustine would repeat this Poltinian phrase on his deathbed. Cf. Possidius, *Vita Augustini* 28: *Non erit magnus magnum putans quod cadunt ligna et lapides et moriuntur mortales* ["He will not be great who thinks it important that wood and rocks should fall, and that mortal beings die"—Trans.].

20. Ambrose, *On Jacob* I, 8, 36: "When the sage struggles with extremely intense suffering, he will not arouse pity; rather, like a light within a lantern, he will show that the strength of his soul continues to shine by itself in the midst of terrible storms and the most furious winds, and that it cannot be extinguished."

21. Ambrose, *On Jacob* I, 8, 39: "If a person accustomed to playing the cithara sees his instrument broken into pieces, with its strings broken, smashed and useless, he will throw it away. He will no longer seek his rhythms there, and will make do with his own voice. So it is with the sage: he will leave the cithara of his body, now useless, on the ground, and will amuse himself within his own heart."

be nothing; soon, Plotinus will be able to sing without a lyre. Still, how could he reproach his body? It was a lyre—and a good one—and it has served him well.

But why is it that we need a body, and why are we forced to leave it behind? Why must there be a sensible world, where struggles and suffering tear people to pieces? Where does evil come from?

Plotinus ardently meditated on these questions, but the reply he gives in his last writings is not a coherent one.

It was in the course of his readings or remembrances of Plato's *Laws* and Stoic treatises on Providence, that Plotinus found the edifying thoughts and maxims of wisdom that elevated his soul as he struggled with suffering, and made him look with serenity at the spectacle—at once terrible and magnificent—of the world he was about to leave.

Evil is not extraneous to the order of the universe; rather, it is the result of this order. Not everything can have the same rank, and the farther things are from the primal Source which is the absolute Good, the more they are deprived of Goodness. Evil, therefore, is nothing other than the privation of Goodness.[22]

To accept the universal order is to accept the existence of degrees of goodness, and, thus, indirectly, to accept evil. We must not criticize the order of the world just because there are consequences in it which seem bad to us:

We are like people who know nothing about painting and yet reproach the artist because he did not put pretty colors everywhere, whereas the artist distributed the appropriate color to each and every spot. Cities, too—even those which have a good constitution—are not made up of equal citizens. It is as if one were to criticize a drama because all the characters in it were not heroes, but it also contained a slave and a foulmouthed hayseed. And yet they make the play complete, and it wouldn't have been any good if you took them away. (III 2, 11, 9–16)

We must, says Plotinus, consent to the order of the world and the laws of the universe, since they emanate from divine Thought, and,

22. Saint Ambrose repeated this point of Plotinus' teaching, in his sermon *On Isaac* VII, 60: "Quid ergo est malitia nisi boni indigentia? ["What else is evil but the lack of the good?"—Trans.] This doctrine was to have a great influence on Saint Augustine, as has been shown by P. Courcelle, 1950, p. 124 n. 4.

ultimately, from the Good. Good and evil, reward and punishment are part of "the nature of things," in other words, the divine order:

> If one group is unarmed, and another is armed, then it is the latter who win. It was not up to the Divinity to intercede in person and fight on behalf of the unwarlike, for the Law states that it is the manly who are saved from wars, and not those who do nothing but pray. It is not those who pray who reap the harvest, but those who till the soil; nor can one be healthy except by looking after one's health. We ought not to whine if bad men get a better harvest, or if things generally go better for them as farmers. . . . If the evil are in power, it is because of the cowardice of their subjects;[23] this is what is just, and it is the contrary state of affairs which would be unjust. Providence must not be such that it makes nothings out of us. If Providence alone were all there were, it would no longer be Providence, for upon whom would it exert providential action? (III 2, 8, 35—9, 3)

Evil is part of the nature of things, and for the sage it is a salutary test. One of Plotinus' first writings had already expressed this idea: "In those whose faculties are too weak for them to be able to know evil by the mere faculty of knowledge, prior to any experience, the experience of evil makes the knowledge of the Good more clear" (IV 8, 7, 15–17).

It is as though mankind could not distinguish good from evil except by experiencing both, and could enjoy goodness only after having gone through the experience of evil. So Plotinus writes, near the end of his life:

> Some things, such as poverty and illness, benefit those who suffer them. Evil, however, contributes something useful to the All: a paradigm of justice.[24] Moreover, it provides, in and of itself, many useful side effects: it wakes us up, and awakens the spirit and intelligence, as we are forced to stand against the inroads of wrongdoing; and it makes us learn how great a good is virtue, by comparison with the evils which are the lot of wrongdoers. Now, it was not for this purpose that evils came about, but since they have come about, the world makes use of them as appropriate. . . . This is a sign of the greatest power: to be able to make good use even of evils. (III 2, 5, 15–24)

23. [Cf. Plato, *Symposium* 182d: "the lust for power of the rulers, and the cowardice of their subjects" (H/T/B).—Trans.]

24. [That is, as Bouillet saw (*Les Ennéades de Plotin,* vol. 2, p. 33): "It gives divine justice the opportunity to be exercised."—Trans.]

Sometimes evil seems to be in the nature of things, while at other times Plotinus considers it a salutary trial; but it also sometimes seems to become, for Plotinus, a spectacle he contemplates with contemptuous indifference.

For him, the sight of human beings hurrying to and fro becomes the puppet dance of which Plato (*Laws* VII, 803–4) had already spoken:

There is a Life full of multiplicity in the universe, and it creates and varies all things as it lives, and it cannot bear not to constantly produce beautiful and well-shaped living toys. The arms of men who attack each other—even though they are mortal, they fight in graceful order, as is done for fun in the Pyrrhic dances[25]—go to show that all mankind's serious concerns are only children's games. . . . Just like on a theater stage, that is how we must consider all murders and rapings and sackings of cities: these are all changes of scenery and costume, acted-out wailings and lamentations. In this world, in each event that happens to us in life, it is not the inner soul, but the outer shadow of a person which laments and grieves; everything it does, it does on the stage of the entire earth. . . . Such are the acts of the person who knows only how to live the lower and outer life, and who does not know that in the midst of his tears, even when they are serious, he is playing children's games. Serious matters should be taken seriously only by a person's serious part; the rest of the person is a mere toy. . . . If you play with them and have a bad experience, at least realize that you have fallen into a children's game, and take off the toy that you are wearing.[26] Even if it is Socrates who is playing, he plays with the outer Socrates. (III 2, 15, 31–59)

Yet what a divine comedy it is! The universal drama has a providential plot. Everyone has a role in the play, and it is the only role that suits him, the only role he would have chosen; better yet, it is the role he *does* choose in the depths of his self. In this absolute drama, there is no difference between the actors and their characters. To act badly is to be a bad character, and a good role is a good performance:

In the true dramatic creation, which is partially imitated by people of a poetical nature, the soul is the actress, and she gets the roles she plays from

25. [On the Pyrrhic dances cf. Strabo 10, 4, 16. Plotinus' source for the simile is Plato, *Laws* 815a.—Trans.]

26. [I.e. the body.—Trans.]

the poet.[27] Just as actors in this world do not receive at random their masks, their costumes, their expensive robes, and their ragged clothes, so it is with the soul herself: she does not receive her fortunes at random, but they, too, are in accordance with reason. If the soul adapts them to herself, she becomes harmonious and coordinates herself with the drama, as well as with the whole of reason. (III 2, 17, 32–39)

If the soul acts badly, however, that too has been foreseen in the play. And the drama is not a whit less beautiful:

A bad sound will be beautiful in relation to the whole, and an unnatural sound will be natural for the universe, although this does not make it any the less an inferior sound. But the soul, as she emits this inferior sound, does not make worse the quality of the whole, just as—to use another image—an evil executioner does not make worse a city governed by good laws; a city has to have its executioner[28]—men such as those are often necessary—and he is in his proper place. (III 2, 17, 83–89)

Just because a soul has a bad part to play does not mean that she herself is irremediably evil. Plotinus steadfastly refuses to concede to the Gnostics that there are souls which are evil by nature. The soul is fundamentally good; it is the inferior part of ourselves—the outer, terrestrial man—who may, when blinded by the body and material things, let himself slide into vice (I 8, 4, 6). But the soul of each human being, in that summit of herself which often remains completely unconscious, is impeccable: "The nature of this [higher] soul in us is separate from all blame for the evil deeds either committed or undergone by man, for these evil deeds have to do with the common animal (i.e., the area where the lower levels of the soul are mixed with the body)" (I 1, 9, 1–3).

This is a theme to which Plotinus' final thought constantly re-

27. [*Para tou poiêtou*. An untranslatable play on words: *poiêtos* means equally "author of a play or poem" and "creator"; in this case, a reference to the world-creating Intellect.—Trans.]

28. Cf. Augustine, *On Order* II 4, 12: "What is there more terrible than an executioner? Is there a soul more cruel and ferocious than his? Nevertheless, the law accords him a necessary place, and he is part of the order of a well-governed city. In himself, he is evil, but in the order of the city, he is the scourge of evil-doers." See also Joseph de Maistre, *Soirées de Saint-Pétersbourg* ["Evenings in Saint Petersburg"—Trans.], First Discourse: "Take this incomprehensible agent (the executioner) away from the world, and in the same instant, order gives way to chaos."

turns. It presupposes the doctrine of the levels of the self, which we set forth in chapter 2. Our true self escapes from suffering, evil, and passions; it even escapes from the astral influences to which some people would have us be subject:

> So, they say, our character comes from the stars; according to our character, our actions; and our passions come from our passionate disposition.[29] What, then, is there left of us? What's left is what we truly are, we to whom Nature has granted dominion even over our passions. Even though we are caught up in such evils through the fault of our bodies, God has given us "virtue, which knows no master." For it is not when we are at peace that we need virtue, but when we would be in danger of falling victim to evils, were it not for virtue. This is why we must "flee from here," "separate" ourselves from those things that have been added on to us, and no longer be that composite, ensouled body in which the nature of the body is predominant. . . . But it is to the other soul, which is not within the body,[30] that belongs the drive towards the upper regions; toward the Beautiful and the Divine, over which no one has power.[31] (II 3, 9, 12–26)

He who lives at this summit of himself dominates destiny, while he who lives on the inferior levels of the self is under the sway of the stars, and is nothing but a fragment of the universe.

One senses that, as death came nearer, Plotinus was striving more and more to reduce himself to his spiritual self and to consider the corporeal life he would soon abandon as totally alien to him.

Plotinus' last, very short treatise is a meditation on death, and a kind of stripped-down summary of his entire philosophy.[32] He takes one last earthly look in the direction of the Good, before definitive contemplation begins: "The Good is not what it is by virtue of its activity or its thought, but by virtue of its pure remaining. . . . We must assume that the Good is that to which all things are attached,

29. [*Hexis pathêtikê*. As Bouillet saw (vol. 1, 1857, p. 179), the "passionate (literally, 'pathetic') disposition" is equivalent to our "animal nature"; cf. *Enn.* III 1, 8–10.—Trans.]

30. [Because the "other soul" is a spiritual entity, it occupies no space and cannot therefore be said to be "in" anything physical.—Trans.]

31. [Again, a patchwork of Platonic quotations. "Virtue which knows no master" comes from the *Republic* 617e; "fleeing from here" from *Theaetetus* 176a-b; "separation" from *Phaedo* 67c.—Trans.]

32. Saint Ambrose translated it almost word for word in his sermon *De bono mortis* ["On the Good of Death"—Trans.], I, 1 and IV, 13–14.

while it itself is not attached to anything. . . . It must remain still, and all other things must turn towards it, as a circle turns towards the center from which its radii emanate" (I 7, 1, 17–24).

He then considers the totality of things which, emanating from the Good, strive to return to it: "How is it that all things turn towards the Good? Inanimate objects turn towards the Soul, and the Soul— through the intermediary of the Spirit—turns towards the Good. Each thing, then, possesses something of the Good, insofar as it is some- how one and existent and participates in Form" (I 7, 2, 1–4).

If even lifeless objects have a trace of the Good, how good must life itself be! Life is a Good, whether it be the life of the soul or life of the Spirit. In particular, life on earth, even though mixed with evil, is a good thing. "But if life is a good for us . . . how can death be any- thing other than an evil?" (I 7, 3, 3–4).

In any case, Plotinus replies, death is not an evil. If, as the Epi- cureans maintained, death is annihilation, then it is not an evil: "It is necessary to *be* something in order to experience evil. But a dead person no longer *is,* or, if he does exist, he is deprived of life[33] and does not suffer any more evil than a rock" (I 7, 3, 5–8).

On the other hand, if one is a Platonist and believes in life after death, death is still a good:

> If life and the soul exist after death, then death is a good, all the more so in that the soul is better able to carry out her proper activities without the body. If she becomes a part of the universal Soul, what kind of evil could affect her there? In general . . . there is no evil for the soul who has main- tained her purity; and if she has not maintained it, then it is not death that is an evil for her, but rather life. Even if there are punishments in Hades, then, once again, it is *life* that is an evil for her, for it is not life and nothing but[34] . . . If one has led a good life, how can death not be an evil? In the case of those whose life is good, it is not good insofar as it is the union of soul and body, but insofar as, through virtue, it defends itself against evil. Thus death is an even greater good.[35] It could perhaps be said that, in and of itself, life

33. [Since life is the necessary precondition for sensation, that which has no life can have no sensations and hence cannot suffer.—Trans.]

34. [The soul's life in Hades is not "life and nothing else," in that it cannot exer- cise the activity proper to it in a free and unimpeded way.—Trans.]

35. [Since it delivers us from the body, and hence from the danger of any further evils (Bouillet).—Trans.]

within the body is an evil, but that, thanks to virtue, the soul can come to be within the Good, not by living the life of the composite [sc. of soul and body], but by separating herself from it already in this life. (I 7, 3, 7–22)

Let us be frank: whoever has read the magnificent treatises which Plotinus, in his maturity, had devoted to the beauty of the world of Forms or to the love of the Good feels a certain disappointment when reading the productions of the end of his life. Porphyry himself had noticed this: "The last nine treatises were written when his strength was failing, the four last ones even more so than the previous five" (V. P. 6, 34–37).

In these last treatises, Plotinus is often satisfied to repeat his own teachings, setting them forth in a very schematic way, as he did in his very first treatise, or else he gives summaries of his readings in Stoicism and Platonism. We find here a great deal of dryness and lack of ornament, and sometimes, as we have seen, even a contemptuous tone.

All this can perhaps be explained by Plotinus' growing detachment from literary form. It is also, perhaps, the sign of a soul growing rigid and unyielding in solitary suffering, as it tries to force itself to consent to reality in its totality, however hard this may be.

☐

Eustochius later told me that he was living in Puteoli at the time, and that when Plotinus was about to die he was late in getting to him. Plotinus said, "I'm still waiting for you," and added that he was trying to make what was divine within him rise up to what was divine in the Universe.[36] At that instant, a serpent came out from under the bed in which he was lying and slid into a hole in the wall,[37] and Plotinus gave his last breath. He was, according to Eustochius, sixty-six years old. (V. P. 2, 23–30)

All of Plotinus is contained within these *ultima verba*.[38] We can see his smiling gentleness: "I'm still waiting for you," he remarked,

36. There is still a great deal of uncertainty amongst specialists as to the exact content of Plotinus' last words. For the latest state of the question, see H.-R. Schwyzer, 'Plotins letztes Wort', *Museum Helveticum* 33 (1976), 85–97. [According to the other view, Plotinus' last words were a recommendation to his disciples: "*Try* to make the divine within *you* rise up. . . .", etc.—Trans.]

37. The soul escaping in the form of a serpent was a widespread popular belief in Antiquity.

38. ["Last words."—Trans.]

as if to say, "I didn't want to die without seeing you again: you, my last friend, the only disciple who stayed with me. But you took your time getting here! I had to postpone my departure because of you!"

We can also feel his sense of the divine presence: "If to philosophize is to learn how to die," he was saying, "I am now carrying out the philosophical act *par excellence*. I'm trying to make whatever is divine within me rise back up to whatever is divine in the universe." As he lay dying, Plotinus did not sum up his "message" in extraordinary terms. We find no allusion to the One, to the Good, or even to the Spirit. His last words were an almost banal phrase, equivalent to "I am giving up my soul to God," expressed in Stoic terminology. It is as if he were saying: "My soul is going back to join the Soul of the World." Yet the totality of Plotinus' writings allows us to glimpse a mystical meaning behind these simple words: Plotinus' soul, made one with the Soul of the universe, is going to contemplate the divine Spirit and its ineffable source, the wholly simple Good. And then we call to mind the strangely beautiful phrases he used to evoke the presence of God: "You have not said, 'I am of such-and-such dimensions,' but you have dropped the 'such-and-such' and have become the All. To be sure, you were already previously the All. . . . When one comes to be someone—that is, by the addition of Not-Being, he is not the All: not until he rids himself of this Not-Being. Thus, you increase yourself when you get rid of everything else, and once you have gotten rid of it, the All is present to you" (VI 5, 12, 18–25).

□

Seventeen centuries now separate us from Plotinus. Modern history is accelerating more and more, sweeping us inexorably away from the sage dying alone in a Campanian villa. An immense abyss has opened up between us and him. And yet, when we read certain pages of the *Enneads*, something within us wakes up; an echo resounds in the depths of ourselves. Bergson was right to speak about the call of the mystics: "They ask for nothing, and yet they receive. They have no need to exhort us. They only have to exist, for their existence is a call."[39]

39. H. Bergson, 1939, p. 30. [Like the English "call," the French word *appel* carries a whole range of connotations, from the prosaic "phone call" (*appel téléphonique*)

Today, however, people are suspicious of the "call" of Plotinus. Is it not deceptive and dangerous, as seductive as the song of the Sirens? Our generation is afraid of being "mystified"; whether Marxist, positivist, Nietzschean, or Christian, we refuse the mirage of the "purely spiritual." We have discovered the power of matter, of that whole lower world that Plotinus considered weak, impotent, and close to nothingness. In the words of Simone Weil, "Food lines. The same action is easier if the moving object is low than if it is higher. Low-flying objects contain more energy than high-flying objects. Problem: how to transfer the energy contained by the low objects to the higher objects?"[40]

This idea was already expressed by Nicolai Hartmann: "The higher the categories of being and of value, the weaker they are,"[41] and by Max Scheler: "That which is inferior is originally in possession of power; that which is superior is impotent."[42] Let Plotinus refuse, if he wishes, to identify himself with the "composite," the "human animal"; we moderns know that it is from this very composite that Plotinus derives the energy which sustains his spiritual activity. We have discovered the power of the social, psychological, biological, and material infrastructures. Marxism and psychoanalysis have taught us about the mechanisms of mystification: a person who thinks he can detach himself from the human condition is nothing but the plaything of inferior motives, and is trying to escape the demands of labor and action.

There is something healthy about this criticism of "pure spirituality." For too long, disguises which served to protect class prejudices, or psychological deficiencies, were taken for authentic values. Nevertheless, I hope to have shown in this work that, despite some of Plotinus' phraseology, his mysticism, in the form in which he lived it, does not appear to have been an escape mechanism. He was just as intensely present to other people as he was to the Spirit.

---

to "appeal," "demand," "summons," "invitation." "*L'appel du général de Gaulle,*" for instance, refers to de Gaulle's proclamation of resistance to the Nazis on June 18, 1940, and may call up, for the French reader, stirring associations of patriotism, duty, and solidarity.—Trans.]

40. S. Weil 1947, p. 3.
41. Quoted in M. Scheler 1951, p. 84.
42. M. Scheler 1951, p. 85.

Above all, the critique of "pure spirituality" must be a prelude to an authentic purification of spiritual life; by no means must it lead to the suppression of an entire area of human reality. As Bergson was well aware, the mystical experience is a universal and extremely significant phenomenon. Even if this phenomenon attains its plenitude only with Christianity, it nevertheless exists, in a highly authentic way, throughout human history. The Plotinian experience is one of the most remarkable examples of this, and if it awakens an echo in us, this is because human reality contains a latent potentiality for the mystic life.

To ignore our material, psychological, or sociological conditioning would indeed be to mystify ourselves. But there is another kind of mystification, just as tragic, although more subtle: it consists in imagining that human life can be reduced to its analyzable, mathematizable, quantifiable, or expressible aspects. One of the great lessons of the philosophy of Merleau-Ponty was to teach us that it is perception—that is, lived experience in the full sense of the term—which gives meaning to scientific representations.[43] Since, however, there is already an inexpressible element within perception itself, this is implicitly to admit that human existence derives its meaning from something inexpressible. Wittgenstein was profoundly conscious of the part played by the inexpressible in the midst of scientific or everyday language:

That which mirrors itself in language, language cannot represent.[44]

There is indeed the inexpressible. This shows itself (but cannot be expressed); it is the mystical.[45]

Mankind is thus in an almost untenable position. The inexpressible makes its appearance, breaking through the comfortable, familiar texture of the everyday. We cannot, therefore, shut ourselves up in the latter, to live within it totally and be satisfied. If, however, we dare to confront the mystery, we will not be able to maintain this attitude. We will have to come back, pretty quickly, to the reassuring obviousness of the everyday. Our inner life will never be entirely

43. Cf. M. Merleau-Ponty 1945, p. 491.
44. L. Wittgenstein 1922, p. 79, proposition 4.121.
45. Ibid., p. 187, prop. 6.522; cf. prop. 4.1212.

unified: it will never be pure ecstasy or pure reason or pure ani-
mality. Plotinus was already well aware of this. He gently accepted
the multiple levels of our being, and all he tried to do was to reduce
this multiplicity as much as possible, by turning his attention away
from "the composite." For him, it was necessary that mankind learn
to tolerate itself.

Today, we are even more inwardly divided than was Plotinian
man. We are still, however, capable of hearing Plotinus' call. There
can be no question of slavishly imitating the spiritual itinerary
of Plotinus here in the late twentieth century; that would be impossible or illusory. Rather, we must consent, with as much courage as
Plotinus did, to every dimension of human experience, and to everything within it that is mysterious, inexpressible, and transcendent.

Postface to the Third Edition

The third edition of this little book appears at a moment in which I am engaged in the formidable task of providing for the public a complete translation, with commentary, of the treatises of Plotinus. Once it is completed—or at least well on the way—the idea I now have of Plotinus may be considerably changed, for one does not understand an author well until the end of the long dialogue one engages with him when translating and commenting on him. At any rate, it seemed to me that the text of this essay, which is now twenty-five years old, and represents a first approximation to the thought of Plotinus, could still be retained without modifications, apart from some details I have pointed out in the footnotes. I have also given up the idea of providing a complete bibliography, since the number of important works devoted to Plotinus has increased considerably in the past few years. Besides, we now possess some excellent bibliographically oriented studies, which I have pointed out at the end of the book.

I have been deeply touched by the testimonies I have received from many readers, telling me of the spiritual benefit they had derived from reading this little volume. They also surprised me, I confess; I am very much aware of the distance separating Plotinus' Platonism from this, our end of the twentieth century. It would seem, therefore, that despite this distance, Plotinus' message has conserved all its power of suffusing light. Doesn't this prove that, above and beyond differences of mentality and civilization, the "call of the mystics" still remains mysteriously alive?

Limours, October 15, 1988

Chronological Biography

205 Birth of Plotinus, probably in Egypt. Perhaps at Lycopolis (V. P. 2, 37).

230–31 At the age of twenty-eight, Plotinus decides to dedicate himself to philosophy, and attends the classes of several famous professors at Alexandria, all of whom disappoint him. (V. P. 3, 7).

232–42 On the advice of a friend, Plotinus attends the classes of Ammonius, and remains for eleven years as his disciple. His fellow-students include Herennius and Origen. This pagan Origen, whom Porphyry mentions several times in his *Life of Plotinus,* must be distinguished from the Christian Origen, the Church Father who was nearly twenty years older than Plotinus.

234 Birth of Porphyry.

243 Plotinus joins the army of the Emperor Gordian in Mesopotamia. In the course of this military expedition, he hopes to meet Persian or Hindu sages.

244 (February/March) Gordian is assassinated by Roman soldiers, partisans of the usurper Philip the Arab. Plotinus has difficulty escaping to Antioch. This kind of *pronunciamento* is very frequent in the third century. Since the death of Alexander Severus (235), the Roman Empire has been going through a severe crisis. Emperors are sometimes chosen by the Senate—this was the case with Gordian—but they are made and unmade by the armies. The fact that Plotinus was able to join Gordian's expedition perhaps allows us to suppose that he had good relations with the Senate, which was well-disposed towards Gordian.

For a more precise chronological table, the reader may consult Richard Goulet, "Le système chronologique de la *Vie de Plotin,*" in L. Brisson et al., 1982, pp. 187–227, especially p. 213.

244   After his Mesopotamian disaster, Plotinus arrives at Rome.

244–53   Plotinus gives lessons to a small number of students, but writes
          nothing.

246   Amelius becomes Plotinus' student. He edits his notes taken dur-
          ing Plotinus' classes.

254   First year of the reign of Gallienus. Plotinus begins to compose
          some treatises (V. P. 4, 10).

263   Porphyry comes to Rome from Athens, where he had been the
          student of Longinus. Although it is summer vacation time,
          Porphyry is able to meet Plotinus (V. P. 5, 4). Porphyry is not im-
          mediately allowed into the school. After a long discussion with
          Amelius, he is won over to one of the points of Plotinian doc-
          trine which he had found difficulty accepting; Plotinus' writings
          are then entrusted to him (V. P. 18, 19).

266   The senator Sabellinus, one of Plotinus' auditors (V. P. 7, 31) is
          consul and colleague of the emperor Gallienus. The latter, as
          well as his wife, the Empress Salonina, hold Plotinus in high re-
          gard (V. P. 12, 1). Plotinus dreams of restoring a ruined town in
          Campania and making out of it the Platonic republic of Pla-
          tonopolis. The project fails, owing to the ill-will of some of the
          Emperor's counselors.

268   Porphyry, suffering from depression, considers committing sui-
          cide. Plotinus advises him to travel, and Porphyry leaves Rome
          for Sicily, where he stays at the home of a certain Probus in Lily-
          baeum (V. P. 11, 11).

268 (Summer)   Assassination of Gallienus; beginning of the reign of
          Claudius II. The first signs of Plotinus' final illness appear (V. P.
          2, 11).

268–9   Departure of Amelius, who leaves Rome to join Longinus at the
          court of Queen Zenobia at Tyre (V. P. 19, 32). The following
          year, Amelius is at Syrian Apamea (V. P. 2, 33).

269   Plotinus leaves Rome and withdraws to the estate of Zethus, six miles from Minturnae in Campania (V. P. 2, 18).

270   Death of Plotinus (V. P. 2, 23).

301   Porphyry writes the *Life of Plotinus,* publishes first edition of the *Enneads* (V. P. 23, 13). Porphyry specifies that he is sixty-eight years old at the time of writing.

Analytical Bibliography

In what order should I read Plotinus?

I. For a partial reading:

a) The indispensable minimum may be found in the treatises I 6 ("On the Beautiful") and VI 9 ("On the Good").

b) For the study of Plotinian mysticism and theology, the essential may be found in VI 7 ("On the Ideas and the Good"),[1] and VI 8 (On the Will of the One").[2]

c) On Plotinus' polemics against the Gnostics, which are crucial for understanding the essence of Plotinian thought, the following treatises ought to be read: III 8 ("On Contemplation"); V 8 ("On Intelligible Beauty"); V 5 ("That the Intelligibles Are Not outside the Intellect"); and II 9 ("Against the Gnostics").

II. For a complete, in-depth study, it seems to me to be indispensable to read the treatises of Plotinus in their chronological order. When he edited his Master's treatises, Porphyry divided them up according to a systematic, arbitrary schema, taking no account of the order in which they had been composed, sometimes chopping them up rather brutally. His goal was to obtain a total of fifty-four treatises, i.e. a product of the perfect numbers six and nine (V. P. 24, 13). Thus the *Enneads,* as we have them today, consist of six groups of nine treatises each. According to Porphyry, each group consists of treatises dealing with a common subject matter: the first *Ennead* corresponds to ethical subjects, the second to subjects dealing with physics, the third to questions about the world in general. The fourth *Ennead* is particularly concerned with the soul, the fifth with the divine Intellect, and the sixth, finally, with the Good or the One (V. P. 24, 16ff.).

From this we can deduce Porphyry's real intentions. The systematic order, which he so artifically introduced, in fact corresponds to the stages of

1. [See now Hadot's translation with commentary, details given below, p. 125.—Trans.

2. [See now the excellent edition, with translation and commentary, by Georges Leroux: *Plotin, Traité sur la liberté et la volonté de l'Un [Ennéade VI, 8 (49)]* (= Histoire des Doctrines de l'Antiquité classique 15), Paris: Librairie Philosophique J. Vrin, 1990.—Trans.]

perfection in spiritual life. Thus, Porphyry classified the treatises of Plotinus in an order corresponding to a division of the parts of philosophy which distinguished three stages in spiritual progress. Morals or ethics were placed at the beginning, to insure that initial purification of the soul which was essential for any further advancement. Next came physics, which completed the process of purification by revealing the vanity of the objects of sense perception. Finally, came the epoptic part—so called after a term used in the Eleusinian Mysteries—otherwise known as metaphysics, which was to provide to the completely purified soul the supreme revelation of the divine mysteries. We find this division of the parts of philosophy in Plutarch (*On Isis and Osiris,* 382d); Theon of Smyrna (*Exposition of Mathematical Matters Useful for the Reading of Plato,* p. 14 Hiller); Clement of Alexandria (*Stromata,* I, 36, 176, 1–2 Stählin), and Origen (*On the Song of Songs,* p. 75, 6 Baehrens), and it was destined to play an important role in Christian mysticism.

However, the systematic order introduced by Porphyry is all the more arbitrary in that most of Plotinus' treatises deal with ethics, physics, and metaphysics at the same time and are not susceptible to being locked up within scholastic classifications. Plotinus' writings were always written for specific occasions; as Porphyry himself indicates, Plotinus "took the subjects [sc. of his treatises] from the problems which happened to come up" (V. P. 5, 60–61).

Fortunately, Porphyry has preserved for us a chronological list of the treatises,[3] which we have every reason to believe is accurate, at least in its broad outlines. It is thus this list which can provide us with the order to follow in our reading of Plotinus. The following table indicates the correspondence between the chronological order of the *Enneads,* and the arbitrary arrangement introduced by Porphyry:

1	I 6	11	V 2	22	VI 4	30	III 8	39	VI 8	46	I 4
2	IV 7	12	II 4	23	VI 5	31	V 8	40	II 1	47	III 2
3	III 1	13	III 9	24	V 6	32	V 5	41	IV 6	48	III 3
4	IV 2	14	II 2	25	II 5	33	II 9	42	VI 1	49	V 3
5	V 9	15	III 4	26	III 6	34	VI 6	43	VI 2	50	III 5
6	IV 8	16	I 9	27	IV 3	35	II 8	44	VI 3	51	I 8
7	V 4	17	II 6	28	IV 4	36	I 5	45	III 7	52	II 3
8	IV 9	18	V 7	29	IV 5	37	II 7			53	I 1
9	VI 9	19	I 2			38	VI 7			54	I 7
10	V 1	20	I 3								
		21	IV 1								

---

3. Porphyry, *Life of Plotinus* 4, 22–6, 38.

By reading the treatises in this order, one will not discover a very marked evolution in Plotinus' thought. Our philosopher is extremely true to himself, even when it comes to style and vocabulary. One will, however, be able to see more clearly what problems occupied him at the different stages of his life, and how certain groups of treatises constitute responses to a precise problem. Some of these groups are as follows:

I. First Period of Plotinus' Literary Activity (Treatises 1–21).

1. First of all, we find a group of investigations on the soul, its immorality, its essence, and its presence within the body. These investigations are carried over from one treatise to another; they discuss certain passages from Plato and take up many arguments traditional in the Platonic refutation of Stoic materialism. These investigations correspond to treatises 2 (IV 7), 4 (IV 2), 6 (IV 8), 8 (IV 9), 14 (II 2: "On Circular Movement," i.e. the movement of the soul), and 21 (IV 1).

2. Some problems raised by the Platonic theory of Ideas and the Aristotelian theory of the Intellect are dealt with in writings 5 (V 9) and 18 (V 7).

3. As early as this first period, Plotinus devotes lengthy discussions to the problems raised by that which is beyond thought, in other words by the One. There are problems concerned with ascent (necessity of going beyond Aristotle's divine Intellect); and with derivation (how does what comes after the One derive from the One). These problems are examined in treatises 7 (V 4), 9 (VI 9), 10 (V 1), and 11 (V 2).

4. One treatise is dedicated to the important—albeit at this period still rather isolated—problem of the nature of matter: 12 (II 4).

5. Another group of treatises deals with the problem of purification by means of virtue and the place of the sage in the hierarchy of beings: is he a god or only a *daimôn*?[4] These are treatises 1 (I 6), 15 (III 4), 19 (I 2), and 20 (I 3).

6. Finally, we have some writings about which it is difficult to say whether they once belonged to more extensive wholes; for example 3 (III, 1), which lacks originality; 13 (III 9), which is a collection of notes; and 17 (II 6).

II. Second Period of Plotinus' Literary Activity (Treatises 22–45).

1. The problem of the presence of the Intelligible within the sensible: treatises 22–23 (VI 4–5).

4. [This term has been subject to a wide variety of translations, from "good genius" to "demon." In Greek thought a *daimôn* was a being intermediary between gods

2. Problems concerning the soul: treatises 27–29 (IV 3–5), to which one should probably add 26 (III 6) and 41 (IV 6), which deal with the problem of the soul's impassability.

3. Anti-Gnostic controversy. This group of treatises, which form one single work, is intended to prove that, contrary to the opinion of the Gnostics, the sensible world is not the willed, intentional product of a Demiurge, but the reflection of the Intelligible world, which contains its raison d'être within itself: 30 (III 8), 31 (V 8), 32 (V 5), and 33 (II 9).

4. It may be that treatises 38 and 39 (VI 7 and 8) are connected to this anti-Gnostic group, since they, too, stress the idea of an Intelligible world which finds its raison d'être within itself. Above all, they insist on the concept of the Good, which is the ultimate cause and absolute freedom.

5. Reflection on the architecture and the characteristic features of the Intelligible world inspire treatises 34 (VI 6), 42–44 (VI 1–3), and 45 (III 7), which study intelligible numbers, the supreme genera of logic, and the question of eternity respectively.

6. Finally, there are some rather brief treatises which, as in the case of Plotinus' first period, are perhaps fragments arbitrarily detached from their original context: these are treatises 25 (II 5), 35 (II 8), 36 (I 5), 37 (II 7), and 40 (II 1).

III. Third Period of Plotinus' Literary Activity (Treatises 46–54).

1. From now on, Plotinus is interested above all in the problem of evil. What is the cause of evil? Should we blame Providence for it, or the soul, or the stars, or matter? These questions are discussed in treatises 47–48 (III 2–3), 51 (I 8), and 52 (II 3).

2. Connected with the problem of evil is that of happiness: how can we endure suffering and still remain happy? The sage, argues Plotinus, is happy because he knows how to distinguish between his purely spiritual soul and the composite of soul and body which is what undergoes suffering. Cf. treatises 46 (I 4), 53 (I 1), and 54 (I 7).

3. One isolated treatise (49 [V 3]) is dedicated to the hierarchy of divine hypostases. It takes up the problems discussed in treatises 7, 9, 10, 11, and 38.

4. Finally, treatise 50 (III 5) presents an allegorical interpretation of the

---

and men, either benevolent or maleficient, often confused with the heroized dead.—
Trans.]

myth of Poros and Penia, as it occurs in Plato's *Symposium*.[5] This treatise constitutes a rather isolated phenomenon within Plotinus' oeuvre.

Where should I read Plotinus?

I. *Plotinus,* with an English translation by A. H. Armstrong (Loeb Classical Library), 7 vols., London/Cambridge, Mass.: William Heinemann/Harvard University Press, 1966–88.

Presented in systematic order, this edition and translation is the product of an eminent Plotinist and is extremely important.

II. For many years, the only widely available modern translation was that of E. Bréhier. Each treatise in Bréhier is preceded by a "Notice," which discusses its plan and situates it within the history of philosophy. The general introduction (vol. 1, pp. i–xxxix) is extremely important, especially concerning questions of literary form and style. The Greek text and translation, however, leave a lot to be desired, and must be used with caution. Last drawback: the treatises are presented in the systematic order arbitrarily introduced by Porphyry.

The project of a complete translation of Plotinus' works into French in chronological order and with commentary, has been undertaken under my direction. Volumes having appeared so far:

Plotin, Traité 38 (VI, 7), Introduction, traduction, commentaire et notes par Pierre Hadot, Paris: Editions du Cerf, 1988.

Plotin, Traité 50 (III, 5), Introduction, traduction, commentaire et notes par Pierre Hadot, Paris: Editions du Cerf, 1990.

III. Hellenists may refer to the magisterial critical editions of Paul Henry and Hans-Rudolf Schwyzer:

a. *Plotini Opera, editio maior,* eds. P. Henry and H.-R. Schwyzer, 3 vols. Paris/Brussels: Desclée de Brouwer/l'Edition Universelle, 1951–73.

For philological reasons, this edition presents Plotinus' writings in the systematic order of the Porphyrian *Enneads.* In Volume 2, there is included an English translation of the "Arabic Plotinus," i.e. the pseudonymous *Theology of Aristotle,* which contains numerous quotations and paraphrases of Plotinian treatises. In Volume 3, one may find the remarkable *Addenda* (pp. 332–410), which represent the most up-to-date state of research on the text of Plotinus.

---

5. [See now the author's French translation with commentary, details given above, section II.—Trans.]

b. *Plotini Opera, editio minor,* eds. P. Henry and H.-R. Schwyzer, 3 vols., Oxford: Clarendon Press, 1964–82.

Compared to the preceding item, this edition contains a reduced critical apparatus, and the Greek text frequently differs, since the editors have, in the meantime, often opted for different readings. In volume 3, pp. 291–325, the reader will find new *Addenda,* which contribute several corrections to Volumes 1 and 2. The most recent corrections have been published by H.-R. Schwyzer, "Corrigenda ad Plotini textum," *Museum Helveticum* 44 (1987), pp. 191–200.

IV. There have also been excellent translations of Plotinus into German, Spanish, and Italian:

a. *Plotins Schriften,* by R. Harder, R. Beutler, and W. Theiler, Hamburg: Verlag Felix Meiner, 1956–71.

This edition comes in six volumes, of which the first five are divided into fascicule a), containing Greek text and German translation, and fascicule b), containing explanatory introductions to each treatise and critical notes. It is an irreplaceable monument. The Greek text is good, although sometimes containing too many conjectures, and the German translation is excellent, while the introductions and plans of each treatise complement, although they do not replace, the "Notices" provided by Bréhier.

Harder/Beutler/Theiler's edition presents Plotinus' works in chronological order, while fascicule Vc, by Richard Harder, gives the text and translation of Porphyry's *Life of Plotinus.* Volume 6 contains indices and concordances, and especially, on pp. 103–75, an "Overview of the Philosophy of Plotinus," by W. Theiler. Together with the article by Schwyzer cited below, this is probably one of the most exact, complete, and profound of all the presentations of the thought of Plotinus. Henceforth it is impossible to study Plotinus without going through this indispensable initiation.

b. *Plotino, Enneadi,* Italian translation and critical commentary by V. Cilento, bibliography (up to 1949) by B Mariën, 3 vols., Bari: Laterza, 1947–49.

This work has maintained its usefulness even today.

c. *Plotino, Enéadas* I–II; III–IV (= Biblioteca Clásica Gredos 57; 88), Spanish translation and notes by J. Igal, Madrid: Editorial Gredos, 1982–85.

The work of an excellent Plotinist, interrupted by his untimely death.

V. Research Tools:

Sleeman, J. H., and G. Pollet, *Lexicon Plotinianum,* Leiden/Louvain: E. J. Brill/Leuven University Press, 1980.

Schwyzer, H.-R., (art.) "Plotinos," *Paulys Realencyclopaedie der classischen Altertumswissenschaft,* vol. 21 (1951), cols. 471–592.

————, *Supplementband* 15 (1978), cols. 311–27.

Excellent bibliographies of Plotinian studies have appeared in the journal *Aufstieg und Niedergang der römischen Welt* (eds. W. Haase and H. Temporini), Part II, Volume 36. 1 (1987):

Pp. 528–70: H. J. Blumenthal, "Plotinus in the Light of Twenty Years' Scholarship, 1951–1971."

Pp. 571–623: K. Corrigan and P. O'Cleirigh, "The Course of Plotinian Scholarship from 1971 to 1986."

References

Bergson, Henri. *Oeuvres*. Textes annotés par André Robinet, introduction par Henri Gouhier. Paris: Presses Universitaires, 1959, 1984⁴. (Partial translation: *The Creative Mind,* trans. Mabelle L. Andison. New York: The Philosophical Library, 1946.)

———. *Les deux sources de la morale et de la religion,* Paris: Presses Universitaires de France, 1939. (Translation: *The Two Sources of Morality and Religion.* New York: Doubleday, 1954.)

Brisson, Luc, Marie-Odile Goulet-Cazé, Richard Goulet, Denis O'Brien, et al. *Porphyre: La vie de Plotin, vol. I: Travaux préliminaires et index grec complet* (= Histoire des doctrines de l'Antiquité classique 6). Paris: Vrin, 1982.

Courcelle, Pierre. *Recherches sur les confessions de Saint Augustin.* Paris: Etudes Augustiniennes, 1950.

Diels, Hermann, and Walther Kranz, eds. *Die Fragmente der Vorsokratiker,* 3 vols. Zurich: Weidmann, 1989¹⁸.

Eckermann, Johann Peter, *Gespräche mit Goethe in den letzten Jahren seines Lebens, 1823–1832,* 2 vols. Berlin/Leipzig/Wien/Stuttgart: Deutsches Verlagshaus Bong and Co., n.d. (Translation: *Eckermann's Conversations with Goethe,* trans. R. O. Moon. London: Morgan, Laird and Co., n.d.)

Jankélévitch, Vladimir. *Henri Bergson.* Paris: Presses Universitaires de France, 1931, 1975².

Merleau-Ponty, Maurice. *La phénoménologie de la perception.* Paris: Gallimard, 1945. (Translation: *The Phenomenology of Perception,* trans. Colin Smith. London: Routledge & Kegan Paul, 1962, repr. 1990.)

Pascal, Blaise. *Oeuvres complètes,* ed. L. Lafuma. Paris: Seuil, 1963. (Translation: *Pascal's Pensées, with an introduction by T. S. Eliot,* trans. by W. F. Trotter. New York: E. P. Dutton and Co., 1958.)

Saint John of the Cross. *The Collected Works of St. John of the Cross,* trans. K. Kavanaugh and O. Rodriguez. Washington, D.C.: Institute of Carmelite Studies, 1979.

Scheler, Max. *La situation de l'homme dans le monde.* Paris, 1951.

Weil, Simone. *La pesanteur de la grâce.* Paris: Plon, 1947.

Wittgenstein, Ludwig. *Tractatus Logico-Philosophicus,* trans. from the German by C. K. Ogden. London/New York: Routledge & Kegan Paul, 1922, repr. 1988.

Index of Plotinian Quotations

[On the mode of citation, see above, p. xiii.—Trans.]

1. [Numbers in parentheses refer to the chronological order in which Plotinus' treatises were composed.—Trans.]

Index